WE.

MW00960629

My name is Rick Chong and I have spent 1000's of hours training people just like you to become adept at the fine art of "slinging" produce.

The Produce Clerk's Handbook will save you so much time and help make your job a breeze. You will become an expert at retailing and handling produce quickly and skillfully.

Produce can be a tough job and sometimes you need all the ammo in your arsenal to make it through another insane day!

THIS HANDY QUICK REFERENCE GUIDE WILL PAY FOR ITSELF IN LESS THAN A DAY!

I have kept the cost of this book inexpensive and affordable. Please respect my Copyright and recommend this book to your co-workers and friends if it has helped you. Thanks in advance.

Visit my web-site for more produce tips and posts on specialty fruit and vegetables at www.produceclerks.com

I welcome all questions and comments, positive and negative. Your feedback will help make the next edition a better tool for everyone.

Please feel free to contact me at:

Rick@ProduceClerks.com

THE PRODUCE CLERK'S HANDBOOK

Rick Chong

ISBN-13: 978-1470013950
ISBN-10: 1470013959

DEDICATION

For Kimlan

CONTENTS

Chapter 1

The Right Tools

Make your job easier by ensuring you have the right tools close at hand; this is the first step in becoming proficient in the produce department.

Cleanliness

Put on a clean apron at the start of your shift and always keep a clean cloth or wad of paper-towel in one of your pockets. Shoppers will routinely eye your hands for cleanliness while you are stocking. A clean apron and hands reflect a clean produce department.

Necessities

Keep necessities like a paring knife, pens, markers, twist-ties, gloves, note-pad, breath mints, band-aids, etc. in your apron pockets. Sometimes the boss or customers will want to chat and breath mints will keep you in good stead.

Produce Carts

Carts come in very handy, allow you to stock without putting extra stress on your back and cut down on trips to the cooler. Keep a cart close-by, easily accessible and the wheels clean.

Pallet Jacks

Pallet jacks are a necessity too. Sometimes it is easier to pull out pallets or bins to setup, instead of just a few cartons. Keep the wheels free of pallet wrap, netting and occasionally lubricate with WD-40.

Walk-in Coolers

Running in and out of the coolers all day long can affect your health. Keep a warm jacket by the cooler door and remember to launder it once in a while.

Relieving Stress

Everybody has their own way of dealing with stress, remember to take your breaks and meals regularly. Even taking just a few minutes to relax and unwind during the day will relieve stress and make you happier and more effective. Don't skip personal time.

Breaking the Ice with Customers

The majority of shoppers are women, sometimes they will be wary of chatting with you and have their guard up. Handing out twist-ties is a great way to break the ice and start a conversation. They are appreciative of the gesture and usually friendly.

Recommending fruit and veggies will help you move extra product and will also build a good repertoire with your customers. Don't deceive shoppers.

Chapter 2

Stocking Techniques

Learning proper stocking techniques will save you headaches and extra work later on. You will spend less time culling displays and repacking old stock.

Table Displays

Using the edge of the table to rest the carton while you are stocking will crush product on display (Diagram 1A) reducing the shelf-life. You will be forced to cull more often, sales will slow and inventory will backup.

Diagram: 1A

Stocking displays in this manner will crush produce on display

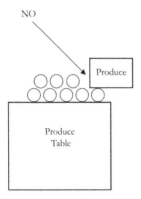

Dumping boxes of produce onto displays will also cause damage. Sometimes this looks like a great short term solution when you are really busy and the product is moving at a good pace. Increased culling does not become an issue.

However the produce has been damaged and will not last once the shoppers gets it home. This can result in store returns, complaints or losing customers.

When you are in a hurry, use your knee as a table to hold up the box (Diagram 1B); this allows both hands to be free to stock the counter quickly.

Diagram: 1B

Correct technique to stock displays

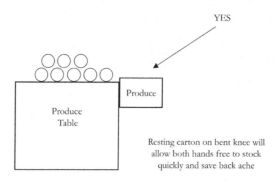

Diagram: 1C

Correct technique to stock displays

Ensure the cart is tight against the produce
table and turn wheels sideways, implement
brake or place one foot against the wheel

YES

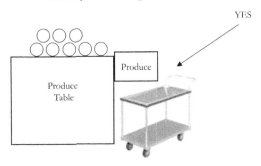

Using a produce-cart (Diagram 1C) saves you from an aching back, bending over all day long is tough on your body. Keep the cart tight against the counter so you are not blocking customers in the aisles. Minimize your reach to fill the display, this saves your body from additional fatigue. Kick the cart-wheels sideways, implement the brake or keep your foot against a wheel so the cart does not shift while you are stocking. Working smart and efficiently becomes second nature as you familiarize yourself with this book and spend time learning the procedures.

Sometimes in the middle of a trip to the cooler to fill your cart, you will be interrupted and forget why you were going there in the first place. Relying on your memory can be counter-productive; you end up wasting time retracing your footsteps trying to remember.

Keep a pen and note-pad in your apron pocket and write down what you need. Making less trips to the cooler makes your job easier.

Diagram: 1D

Correct technique to stock displays

Resting carton on top of empty boxes will allow both hands free to stock quickly and save your back from aching

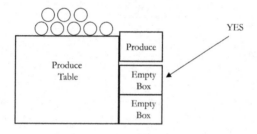

If a produce-cart is not available, try stacking empty apple boxes or banana boxes (Diagram 1D) against the produce counter and place your full box on-top. This allows you to fill displays without having to bend over and put stress on your back. Make sure the boxes are clean and do not smell.

Bin Displays

Bigger displays mean bigger sales (Diagram 2A). A typical table display is wide enough to accommodate 1-2 shoppers, whereas a bin display has 4 facings and can accommodate up to 6 shoppers at one time.

Diagram 2A:

Bin displays allow mulitple shoppers at one time

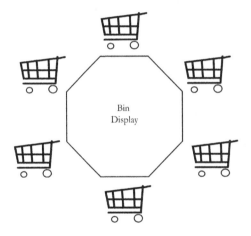

Bin displays will increase sales by at least 200 - 300% and it's a great way to get rid of extra stock. Make sure the display looks good, the retail price is attractive and the signage is visible to shoppers.

Diagram 2S:

Rotating stock

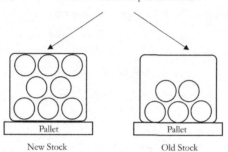

Place old stock on top of new stock

New Stock   Old Stock

When restocking pull out a new full bin with a pallet jack and put the old bin stock on top (Diagram 2S). Product is constantly being rotated and less culling will be required.

If you are running low on inventory, the bin stock should be transferred to a table display and the bin used for something else; or dummy the bin (Diagram 2B) to keep the display looking good.

Remember to visually inspect your displays from a shopper's perspective once in a while. Ensure key bin displays are not hidden and are featured prominently.

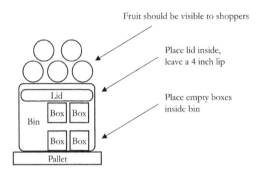

Diagram 2B:

Correct procedure to dummy a bin

Fruit should be visible to shoppers

Place lid inside, leave a 4 inch lip

Place empty boxes inside bin

Diagram 2B:

During slow periods use dummied bin displays to keep shrink low, which means less culling and repacking.

Dummy an empty bin using strong banana or cantaloupe type cartons inside the bin and place the bin lid on top. Make sure you have a 4 inch lip or else the fruit will fall onto the floor. Build a few reusable dummied bins when it's slow and keep them in the backroom for future use.

If the only bins you have available to use look ugly, try stapling empty onion sacks around the outside of the bin to add some color and hide the fact.

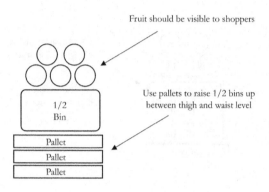

Diagram 2C:

Correct procedure to raise 1/2 bins

Fruit should be visible to shoppers

1/2 Bin

Use pallets to raise 1/2 bins up between thigh and waist level

Pallet

Pallet

Pallet

Diagram 2C:

Receiving fruit in bins makes your job easier. Simply pull off the lid, top off the display and it's ready to go. If you are using ½ bins you will need to raise the bins up with extra pallets underneath. The bins should be raised to between thigh to waist level.

Remember the majority of your shoppers are women; they are typically smaller with a shorter reach. Always try to build your displays with this tidbit of information in the back of your mind. Building a shopper-friendly produce department sometimes takes a little bit of ingenuity and common sense.

Chapter 3

Display Techniques

<u>Ordered & Unordered Displays</u>

There are two methods to displaying produce…
"Ordered" and "Unordered". Both methods should be
implemented depending on the commodity you are
working with.

Diagram: 3A

Ordered and Unordered Table Displays

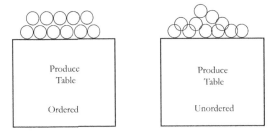

Produce displayed using the "unordered" method sells much better and takes less time to stock. Displaying produce using the "ordered" method can sometimes hampers sales. The produce looks too perfect, shoppers are often afraid of spoiling the display and it can be difficult to pull from the display without toppling the upper layers. Leaving you to pick up spilled produce off the floor.

Commodities like pineapple, melons, bananas, cauliflower, clamshells and bags fare better using the "ordered" method. While apples, oranges, tomatoes, onions, etc. move much better when displayed using the "unordered" method. You need to assess the condition of the produce when you are stocking and decide if it is too fragile to be displayed using the "unordered" method.

Minimizing Shrink and Culls

No one likes having to repack or cull bad produce. Minimize this chore by managing the size of your table displays.

Heaping displays during busy times creates more work for yourself later, having to cull the same displays twice as hard. Try widening out on key items instead (Diagram 3B), this works great. Your section becomes much easier to manage.

During slow times you can build 2nd displays of hard items that are not significantly affected by spending long periods on the tables (kiwi, onions, garlic, squash, etc.) and reduce key perishables.

You minimize shrink and spend less time culling and repacking bad fruit. 2nd displays can be moved and consolidated with their parent whenever required.

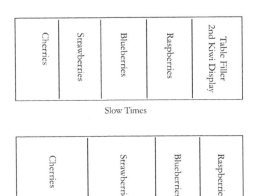

Diagram 3B

Keep highly perishable displays small when its slow, widen out these displays during peak times

Slow Times

Peak Times

Dummying Table Displays

Learning to improvise on the fly is one of the attributes that makes a great Produce Clerk. Today we have all makes of produce containers available to help make the produce department look first-rate. However we do not always have the right equipment at hand and sometimes we need to improvise.

Tomato, grape and avocado type boxes make perfect dummy displays. Save enough empty boxes to build these displays for weak, slow moving, and highly perishable commodities (dragon fruit, peaches, shallots, jicama, etc.).

Dummying displays will reduce culls and repacking. Your produce section will look full, which improves sales. Turn empty cartons upside down or use tomato lids to dummy your empty boxes. The white produce pads you receive in boxes of apples, eggplant, peaches, pears, etc. can be used as a cushion when you setting up your table displays (Diagram 3C). Make sure the boxes, lids and pads are clean and do not smell bad.

Diagram 3C

Building a Dummied Display

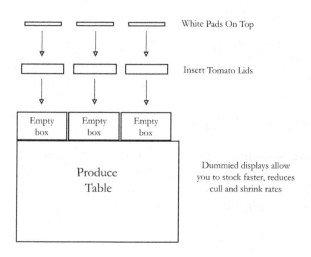

14

Wet Counters

The wet counter is perfect for lettuces and other veggies that require constant hydration. Although over-watering can have just as significant an impact as not spraying.

You do not want to have water-logged vegetables on display. It's important that the display counters are set at the proper angle, water run-off is not blocked and is functioning properly. Ensure the timer is set within the parameters you feel are right for your climate. Experiment if you are not sure.

Close the valves of overhead sprayers for packaged produce displays (mushrooms, herbs, alfalfa sprouts, etc.). Green and yellow beans especially should not be sprayed, they will turn rusty.

We will get into the handling of individual wet counter veggies in the "Vegetables" chapter of this book.

Wet Tables

If you are using wet tables to feature high volume veggies, the tables should be adequately iced beforehand. Ensure the drains in the tables are not blocked or you will have water all over your floors. Keep a water spray-bottle close at hand to occasionally spray and refresh the top layers of the veggie displays.

Vegetable rotation is very important on wet tables. The produce will begin to deteriorate and smell otherwise. If you are sharing a produce section with others, make sure you are all rotating in the same manner and direction.

Chapter 4

Checklists/Plan-o-grams

Checklists and plan-o-grams can save you at least a couple of hours every day. Staying organized is easy once you develop a routine.

Checklist Example 1:

DATE:	DONE
MY MORNING CHECKLIST	
Turn on coffee maker	Y
Apron / knife / pen / notebook / twist ties	Y
Turn on produce counter lights	Y
Check Walk-in cooler temperature	Y
Check produce quality of displays	Y
Stock tables and refill existing displays	
Put out roll bags / twist ties on displays	Y
Put out sample containers / toothpicks	
Check to see if we are heavy on anything	Y
Fix any quality problem on displays	
NOTES:	
Paul will be late today, cover his section too	
Need to push Watermelon today	
No strawberries till Friday	

Most supermarkets have employee checklists that need to be adhered to and checked on a daily basis. It's a great idea to make up your own checklist too, something that works for you. You will be surprised how much time you can save everyday by using checklists.

Again…you are not relying solely on your memory to ensure important tasks are getting done. When you are extra busy, called away unexpectedly or go on break; it is easy enough to hand your checklist over to a co-worker to complete in your absence. Once you have your checklist(s) drawn up to your liking, make plenty of extra copies for future use.

Checklist Example 2:

10 AM MORNING	QUALITY CHECKLIST	
PRODUCT	DATE:	DONE
Golden Delicious	Old stock waxy, bag up	Y
Cauliflower	Black spotting - Trim	
Bok Choy	Trim butts	Y
Cabbage	Leaves yellow - Trim	
Romaine Lettuce	Sleeve	Y
W. Potatoes	Turning green - Rotate	Y
Baby Potatoes	Bags wet - Rebag	Y
Green Leaf	Small, put 2 in a bunch	Y
NOTES:		
Raspberries 3 days old, check when putting up		
Peaches taste great be sure to offer samples		Y
Green Beans starting to wilt, need to move		

The Produce Clerk's Handbook

Plan-o-grams

Diagram 4A: One method of utilizing Plan-o-grams

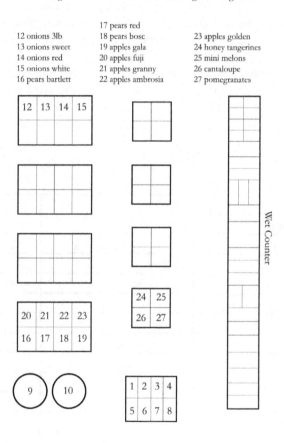

12 onions 3lb
13 onions sweet
14 onions red
15 onions white
16 pears bartlett

17 pears red
18 pears bosc
19 apples gala
20 apples fuji
21 apples granny
22 apples ambrosia

23 apples golden
24 honey tangerines
25 mini melons
26 cantaloupe
27 pomegranates

Week 34 / Tom's Section

Plan-o-grams will save you so much time, you will not know how you worked without them. Usually they are prepared by the Produce Manager and handed out accordingly.

Breaking up the color in the produce department effectively is very important. Too many reds or greens thrown together can make your section look like an eye-sore instead of a work of art.

If plan-o-grams are not already being implemented at your store, take a pen or pencil and try drawing one up yourself. Key items should be displayed in the busier sections of the produce department, while less important commodities are displayed in secondary locations.

Experimenting is the key to implementing effective plan-o-grams. Some people like to work solely with colors, while others break up the categories into round, long, greens, veggies, fruit, ethnic, etc. Putting your ideas down on paper and visualizing your plan-o-gram before it is completed is a great way to utilize this method.

If only one plan-o-gram is being used to setup the entire produce department, it's a good idea to color code assigned produce sections with highliter markers; the plan-o-gram will be easier to read. Make photocopies for everybody.

Eventually you will want to draw up a good floor plan schematic to use on an ongoing basis. Keep a blank master copy on file and print off copies whenever you need them. This will save you lots of time and shows a higher level of professionalism.

Chapter 5

Receiving & Inspecting

Receiving poor quality produce can be just the start of a bad day if it is not caught and proper store protocols followed. Otherwise it will mean more work for you and everyone else in your department, and your customers will not be happy either.

Diagram 5A:

Notice different pack dates, lot and grower numbers

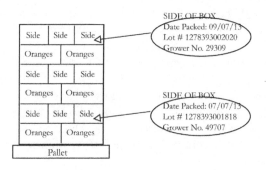

Inspect both lots, unscrupulous shippers often put old stock on the bottoms of pallets to get rid of it

You should feel confident and at ease when you are receiving and inspecting produce. Develop a routine and change it up once in a while as you become more adept.

Whenever possible, produce should be inspected at waist-high level. Try not to put undue stress on your back. Use a produce-cart, stack a few empty banana boxes to use as a table, or something similar.

<u>Pallets</u>

Pallets should arrive properly wrapped, strapped or both. This is a good sign that proper procedure was being followed at origin. Product that has shifted on the pallets is usually caused by the truck driver taking a corner too quickly or applying the brakes too hard.

Diagram 5B:

Crushed and Damaged Boxes

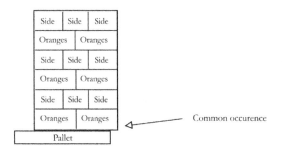

Product has shifted off pallet, inspect
botom layers for crushing and damage

The procedure outlined in Diagram 5C will save you the trouble of having to restack pallets. The majority of the time this procedure can be used quite effectively.

Diagram 5C:

Procedure to correct shifted pallets

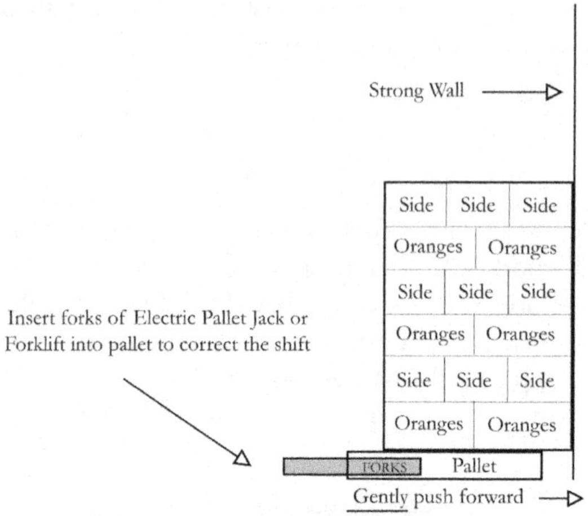

Strong Wall ⟶ ▷

Side	Side	Side
Oranges		Oranges
Side	Side	Side
Oranges		Oranges
Side	Side	Side
Oranges		Oranges

Insert forks of Electric Pallet Jack or
Forklift into pallet to correct the shift

△

| FORKS | Pallet |

Gently push forward ⟶ ▷

Signs of sweating or condensation on the pallet wrap is an indication the produce was sitting out at room temperature too long; or the truck driver had his reefer turned off to save fuel. In this situation, you need to inspect the pallet(s) closely and check the pulp temperatures. If you decide to accept the shipment, record your concerns on the Bill of Lading in case a claim is required later on.

Chilling is also a common problem when you are receiving produce. The truck reefer can easily chill some types of fruit and veggies if they are loaded too close to the reefer. Apricots, asparagus, strawberries and cherries are just a few of the commodities that chill easily. Either by the truck reefer or the cooler fans at the warehouse blowing directly onto the products. Placing a cardboard liner (Diagram 5D) on top of the pallet will prevent this.

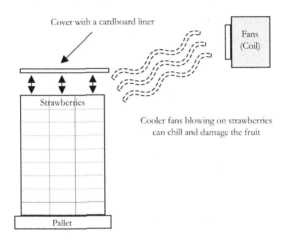

Diagram 5D:

Truck reefers and cooler fans can damage fruit

Cover with a cardboard liner

Fans
(Coil)

Strawberries

Cooler fans blowing on strawberries
can chill and damage the fruit

Pallet

Sometimes your level of expertise will be challenged by truck drivers, shippers and growers. Understanding the causes that affect quality lends you a level of credible professionalism that cannot be argued.

As outlined in Diagram 5A, always remember to check the Date packed, Lot Number and Grower Number. Often unscrupulous shippers will retag old product with new labels and/or put old stock on the bottom of pallets, hoping you will be too dumb to notice or lazy to check. Rejecting shipments with an accumulation of more than 10% defects is a guideline only, use your own judgment.

Forklifts / Power Jacks

Forklifts and power jacks (electric pallet jacks) make the perfect tools to effectively unload, receive and put away your produce orders. You can save yourself several hours of heavy lifting a week.

Learning to use this equipment is quite easy and maintenance is very minimal. You may be required to take a forklift class before you are certified to drive this machinery. Besides recharging the batteries usually once daily, you need to check the water level in the batteries every couple of weeks and refill whenever necessary.

Having scheduled deliveries and/or mandating drivers must call ahead to notify you of their ETA is a real godsend. This allows you ample time to ensure the equipment is charged and ready-to-use.

Ask drivers to help you restack boxes, unload or put away pallets in the cooler. The old saying "You scratch my back and I scratch yours" comes into play and means… I will occasionally let the odd mistake slide without consequence. It's always wise to be friendly and non-confrontational. Don't be a hardass unless all else fails.

Chapter 6

Storage

Using proper storage methods means less culling and repacking. There is nothing worse than having to work through bad, smelly produce.

<u>Refrigerated Produce</u>

Remove pallet wrap (plastic) to allow the produce to breathe after it has been received and accepted. Do not leave discarded pallet wrap or straps lying around, it is very common for coworkers to trip and hurt themselves.

Blocking the entrance of the cooler will make your job much harder. It should be easily accessible for produce-carts, pallet jacks and the forklift too if possible.

There should be designated areas allotted for each commodity; this makes it very easy to locate items. You can waste a lot of time in an disorganized cooler looking for a single box of eggplant. Also designate pallet spaces for weekly specials (always in the same locations).

As previously shown in Diagram 5D, some commodities cannot sustain the constant blowing of the cooler fans upon them (mushrooms, raspberries, apricots, herbs, etc.). Usually these types of commodities are received in open tray-pack cartons or have large side vents. It's wiser to store closed boxes (apples, oranges, celery, in this area of the cooler. If you are short of space, cover the top of the pallet with a cardboard liner to shield it.

Diagram 6A;

Produce Cooler Schematic

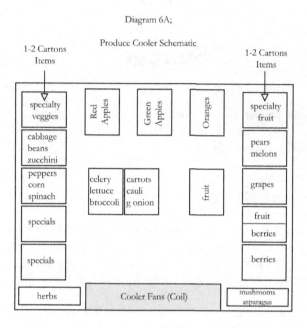

Even using time proven methods to keep your cooler organized is not easy if everyone is not on the same page. Produce begins to rot, the cooler starts to smell and no one wants to be the cleanup guy.

Remember to leave sufficient room in the cooler to put away table stock at closing time. Use produce-carts and pallets whenever possible and bins can be pulled straight into the cooler without fuss.

Non-refrigerated Produce

Commodities like avocados, bananas, mangos and tomatoes should be stored at 50F/10C to room temperature; depending on ripeness and should never be refrigerated. Remove or open lids if the fruit is ripe.

Many fruits and veggies sell better when they are sold on the riper side. Commodities like cantaloupe, pears and nectarines can be left out to ripen and later put into the cooler once the desired ripeness has been reached (Pineapple do not ripen after they have been harvested).

Diagram 6B:

Fruit naturally produces ethylene gas which induces ripening

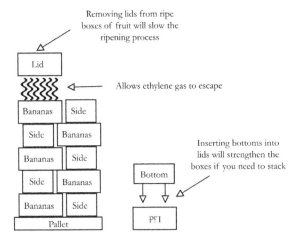

Plastic pallet wrap acts as an insulator and is a great ripening method. Heat and ethylene gas become trapped within the pallet and quicken the ripening process. Once the desired ripeness has been reached, the pallet wrapped should be removed and discarded.

Most supermarkets have a designated back-room area for non-refrigerated produce. The area should be kept clean and free of debris or you will attract mice, cockroaches and other unwanted guests.

Ripe fruit emits a nice aroma, overripe fruit does not. When your back-room begins to smell like fruit, it's time to move the product out; exceptions to this rule are avocados, watermelon, honeydew, etc. These types of fruit need to be checked daily by pressing your thumbs against the rinds for softness. Honeydew in particular will also turn a deep yellow or the rind will turn translucent as it ripens.

Although proper rotation must be adhered to, the exception to the rule is ripe fruit. Ripe fruit should always be placed at the top and front of displays regardless of when the product was received.

Proper storage and ripening methods for individual fruit and veggies will be addressed in the next two chapters titled Chapter 7 "Fruit" and Chapter 8 "Vegetables".

Chapter 7

Fruit

(In alphabetical order)

In this chapter we will discuss the standard pack sizes, weights, and grades of individual fruit. Including displaying and handling suggestions, receiving and storage.

It is impossible to include every variety of fruit grown on planet Earth in this produce manual; it would become too big and hefty and no longer be a convenient, pocket-sized handbook. Also, because it is not needed.

Specialty produce items will be added to my website and can be freely accessed anytime with an internet connection.

I have bought, sold and retailed hundreds of fruit and veggies throughout my produce career, there are many specialty items and varieties I will not include on my website unless requested by you.

The sheer volume of specialty items I have worked with in the last 30 years is well over 400 items i.e. South Americans grow, market and sell yellow passion fruit, while Asians prefer the purple variety. Italians love to eat the hachiya (pointy) persimmons soft and overripe, while Asians eat the fuyu (flat) variety hard like apples. Don't get me started on the differences of figs.

Please email me if you cannot find an answer on my website or would like to leave a comment or feedback.

Apples Overview

Grades: Ex-Fancy | No.1 | Fancy | Commercial | Orchard Run
Sizes: 36 | 48 | 56 | 64 | 72 | 80 | 88 | 100 | 113 | 125 | 138 | 150+
Cartons: 18kg/40# Standard | 20kg/44# Heavy Pack
Bags: 1.36kg/3# | 2.27kg/5# | 3.64kg/8# | 4.54kg/10#
Bins: 182kg/400# | 364kg/800#
Store: Optimum Temperature +1C/33F

Apples is the biggest produce category by sales and volume (although it is sometimes beaten by bananas), and has the biggest impact in the Produce Department.

Apples are often overlooked during the hustle and bustle of maintaining a clean and stocked Produce Department.

Apples and other staples like oranges, grapes, potatoes, tomatoes and onions are the life's blood of your Produce Department. Everybody eats them and they are all very profitable categories. Maintaining nice displays will keep profits healthy and the boss happy. Less stress for you!

During summer and fall harvests, apples are picked, packed and shipped fresh from orchards, fruit cooperatives and packing houses. In winter months however, regular storage fruit becomes waxy, dull and stale tasting. Good quality fruit is pulled from specially regulated rooms called "CA" (controlled atmosphere) rooms to meet demand. Apple boxes should have "CA" stamped on the side of the box to ensure you are receiving good quality. CA rooms regulate the amount of oxygen and have ethylene gas scrubbers to dramatically extend the life of the apples.

Like avocados, bananas, and tomatoes… apples are huge producers of ethylene gas which induces the ripening process. Storing cut flowers near high ethylene gas producing fruit or veggies will halve the flower's shelf-life. Even if they sell quickly, the flowers will not last long once your customer gets them home and puts them in a vase.

Washington State is the biggest apple producer and there are many grades available. Most Supermarkets carry "Extra Fancy" grade. The quality is high, they have great color and there is very little waste or culls.

During harvest however, consumers prefer unpolished apples (orchard run), although supermarkets rarely list this grade. Shrink can be horrendous. Typically the saying is… Good growers… good fruit; Bad growers… bad fruit. Growers that take pride in what they grow do not purposely put culls, hail-marked, bruised or rotten apples in their cartons or bins. Although a small percentage will get by because we rely on machinery and human interaction to pack the fruit and neither are perfect.

Unpolished fruit can be purchased quite cheap in half-bins. Sales can increase by 100-200%. If your store is selling unpolished apples, you should be aware that cashiers usually have a problem identifying apples that do not have PLU stickers. You need to take a sample to the checkouts and show cashiers how to identify the apple variety. Leave a sample at the checkouts.

New Zealand, Chile and China are a few of the major apple producers that ship "new crop" apples during winter months and the differences in taste and quality is quite noticeable. New crop apples will increase sales.

Bitter Pit

Bitter Pit can have a big impact on your apples sales and produce shrink (black and brown spotting). It spreads quite rapidly and can infect unaffected fruit in less than a day.

This "disorder" is caused by a calcium deficiency, learn to recognize this problem when you are receiving new shipments or at the onset in-store (photos can be viewed at www.produceclerks.com). Save yourself headaches and unnecessary extra work.

Apple varieties affected by bitter pit:

- JONAGOLD
- GOLDEN DELICIOUS
- RED DELICIOUS
- GRANNY SMITH
- BRAEBURN
- FUJI
- ROYAL GALA
- MCINTOSH
- SPARTAN

New Varieties

As production increases and the cost of growing newer varieties drops, we see consumers tastes adapting to these newer varieties.

Honey crisp, ambrosia and pacific rose apples are just a few of the "newer" varieties that are stealing away shoppers with their fantastic flavor and eye appeal. Make sure you always give new varieties a chance and offer samples to build new sales and keep shrink low. Customer feedback is important.

Old Varieties

Old varieties like red delicious and braeburn have become dogs. Quite often taking up valuable table space to serve a very small segment of your traffic. If you are throwing out more than you are selling I suggest cutting your display in half and giving more room to better selling varieties.

Apples Ambrosia

Grades: Ex-Fancy | No.1 | Fancy | Commercial | Orchard Run
Sizes: 36 | 48 | 56 | 64 | 72 | 80 | 88 | 100 | 113 | 125 | 138 | 150+
Cartons: 18kg/40# Standard | 20kg/44# Heavy Pack
Bags: 1.36kg/3# | 2.27kg/5# | 3.64kg/8# | 4.54kg/10#
Bins: 182kg/400# | 364kg/800#
Store: Refrigerated | Optimum Temperature +1C/33F

Remarks: Ambrosia are big sellers and can be left out on display for 3-4 days with little impact. Good quality fruit should be very firm and have a minimum of 50-70% red color. All growing regions can produce excellent quality. Ambrosia means "Food of the Gods".

Displaying: Similar to the gala variety and very easy to handle. Red side should face up to maximize eye appeal. Turn apples sideways to prevent stem punctures. Displaying apples under hot light fixtures can turn them waxy and sales will drop off. Sampling can increase sales by +50%. Cull (remove) soft, waxy and bruised fruit. Bag up and sell at a discount or use for samples. Decayed fruit should be thrown out.

Receiving: If available, check the Lot Number, Grower Number and Packing Date on the boxes. Open boxes and inspect the fruit. Stems should be green or brown, not black or shrivelled. Watch out for cracks around the stem bowl. Look for bruises, brown spotting, decay and mold. Firmly press your thumb against the surface for excessive softness. Reject soft apples and shipments in general with an accumulation of more than 10% defects.

Apples Braeburn

Grades: Ex-Fancy | No.1 | Fancy | Commercial | Orchard Run
Sizes: 36 | 48 | 56 | 64 | 72 | 80 | 88 | 100 | 113 | 125 | 138 | 150+
Cartons: 18kg/40# Standard | 20kg/44# Heavy Pack
Bags: 1.36kg/3# | 2.27kg/5# | 3.64kg/8# | 4.54kg/10#
Bins: 182kg/400# | 364kg/800#
Store: Refrigerated | Optimum Temperature +1C/33F

Remarks: Braeburn have become slow movers as shoppers switch to newer and more flavorful varieties. They can be left out on display for 3-4 days with little impact. Good quality fruit should be super hard and have a minimum of 50-70% red color. All growing regions can produce excellent quality.

Displaying: Very easy to handle. Red side should face up to maximize eye appeal. Turn apples sideways to prevent stem punctures. Displaying apples under hot light fixtures can turn them waxy and sales will drop off. Sampling will increase sales marginally. Cull soft, waxy and bruised fruit. Bag up and sell at a discount or use for samples. Throw out decayed fruit.

Receiving: If available, check the Lot Number, Grower Number and Packing Date on the boxes. Open boxes and inspect the fruit. Stems should be green or brown, not black or shrivelled. Watch out for cracks around the stem bowl. Look for bruises, bitter pit, decay and mold. Firmly press your thumb against the surface for excessive softness. Reject soft apples and shipments in general with an accumulation of more than 10% defects.

Apples Cameo

Grades: Ex-Fancy | No.1 | Fancy | Commercial | Orchard Run
Sizes: 36 | 48 | 56 | 64 | 72 | 80 | 88 | 100 | 113 | 125 | 138 | 150+
Cartons: 18kg/40# Standard | 20kg/44# Heavy Pack
Bags: 1.36kg/3# | 2.27kg/5# | 3.64kg/8# | 4.54kg/10#
Bins: 182kg/400# | 364kg/800#
Store: Refrigerated | Optimum Temperature +1C/33F

Remarks: Native to Washington State, Cameo can be left out on display for 2-3 days with little impact. Wide range of quality standards, good quality fruit should be firm and have a minimum of 50-70% red color. Discovered by chance in 1987 by the Caudle family.

Displaying: Sometimes difficult to handle. Red side should face up to maximize eye appeal. Turn apples sideways to prevent stem punctures. Displaying apples under hot light fixtures can turn them waxy and sales will drop off. Taste better than they look, sample to improve sales. Cull soft, waxy and bruised fruit. Bag up and sell at a discount or use for samples. Throw out decayed fruit.

Receiving: If available, check the Lot Number, Grower Number and Packing Date on the boxes. Open boxes and inspect the fruit. Stems should be green or brown, not black or shrivelled. Watch out for soft, waxy fruit, low color and bitter pit. Look for bruises, decay and mold. Firmly press your thumb against the surface for excessive softness. Reject soft apples and shipments in general with an accumulation of more than 10% defects.

Apples Fuji

Grades: Ex-Fancy | No.1 | Fancy | Commercial | Orchard Run
Sizes: 36 | 48 | 56 | 64 | 72 | 80 | 88 | 100 | 113 | 125 | 138 | 150+
Cartons: 18kg/40# Standard | 20kg/44# Heavy Pack
Bags: 1.36kg/3# | 2.27kg/5# | 3.64kg/8# | 4.54kg/10#
Bins: 182kg/400# | 364kg/800#
Store: Refrigerated | Optimum Temperature +1C/33F

Remarks: Big sellers and a favorite with Asians, fuji can be left out on display for 3-4 days with little impact. Good quality fruit should be super hard and have a minimum of 50-70% red color. Most regions produce excellent quality.

Displaying: Bruise easily because of their firmness. Red side should face up to maximize eye appeal. Turn apples sideways to prevent stem punctures. Displaying apples under hot light fixtures can turn them waxy and sales will drop off. Sampling can increase sales by +50%. Cull soft, waxy and bruised fruit. Bag up and sell at a discount or use for samples. Throw out decayed fruit.

Receiving: If available, check the Lot Number, Grower Number and Packing Date on the boxes. Open boxes and inspect the fruit. Stems should be green or brown, not black or shrivelled. Watch out for cracks around the stem bowl. Look for bruises, bitter pit, decay and mold. Firmly press your thumb against the surface for excessive softness. Fruit with "watercores" (liquid cores) is okay and actually much sweeter (picked after the frost). Reject soft apples and shipments in general with an accumulation of more than 10% defects.

Apples Golden Delicious

Grades: Ex-Fancy | No.1 | Fancy | Commercial | Orchard Run
Sizes: 36 | 48 | 56 | 64 | 72 | 80 | 88 | 100 | 113 | 125 | 138 | 150+
Cartons: 18kg/40# Standard | 20kg/44# Heavy Pack
Bags: 1.36kg/3# | 2.27kg/5# | 3.64kg/8# | 4.54kg/10#
Bins: 182kg/400# | 364kg/800#
Store: Refrigerated | Optimum Temperature +1C/33F

Remarks: Usually shipped green, Golden sell much better when they are yellow and have some red blush. They can be left out on display for 1-2 days with little impact. A "chance seedling" discovered in West Virginia in 1891.

Displaying: Golden bruise easily at the picking and packing stages and on display. Refrigerating at night is known to lessen bruise marks; near close let displays run down. Display yellow apples on top to maximize eye appeal and turn sideways to prevent stem punctures. Displaying apples under hot light fixtures can turn them waxy and sales will drop off. Sample when possible. Cull soft, waxy and bruised fruit. Bag up and sell at a discount or use for samples. Throw out decayed fruit.

Receiving: If available, check the Lot Number, Grower Number and Packing Date on the boxes. Open boxes and inspect the fruit. Stems should be green or brown, not black or shrivelled. Watch out for cracks around the stem bowl. Look for bruises, bitter pit, decay and mold. Firmly press your thumb against the surface for excessive softness. Reject soft apples and shipments in general with an accumulation of more than 10% defects.

Apples Granny Smith

Grades: Ex-Fancy | No.1 | Fancy | Commercial | Orchard Run
Sizes: 36 | 48 | 56 | 64 | 72 | 80 | 88 | 100 | 113 | 125 | 138 | 150+
Cartons: 18kg/40# Standard | 20kg/44# Heavy Pack
Bags: 1.36kg/3# | 2.27kg/5# | 3.64kg/8# | 4.54kg/10#
Bins: 182kg/400# | 364kg/800#
Store: Refrigerated | Optimum Temperature +1C/33F

Remarks: Granny sales are generally limited, customers usually come to the supermarket already planning to buy this variety. They can be left out on display for 3-4 days with little impact. Red blush is considered a defect. All growing regions can produce excellent quality. Originating from Australia in 1868 and named after Maria Ann Smith.

Displaying: Easy to handle, turn apples sideways to prevent stem punctures. Displaying under hot light fixtures will turn this variety waxy and sales will drop off. Sampling does not increase sales, although adding blurbs to retail signage like "perfect for pies" or "crunchy" can. Cull soft, waxy and bruised fruit. Bag up and sell at a discount or use for samples. Throw out decayed fruit.

Receiving: If available, check the Lot Number, Grower Number and Packing Date on the boxes. Open boxes and inspect the fruit. Stems should be green or brown, not black or shrivelled. Watch out for cracks around the stem bowl. Look for bruises, bitter pit, decay and mold. Firmly press your thumb against the surface for excessive softness. Reject soft apples and shipments in general with an accumulation of more than 10% defects.

Apples Honey Crisp

Grades: Ex-Fancy | No.1 | Fancy | Commercial | Orchard Run
Sizes: 36 | 48 | 56 | 64 | 72 | 80 | 88 | 100 | 113 | 125 | 138 | 150+
Cartons: 18kg/40# Standard | 20kg/44# Heavy Pack
Bags: 1.36kg/3# | 2.27kg/5# | 3.64kg/8# | 4.54kg/10#
Bins: 182kg/400# | 364kg/800#
Store: Refrigerated | Optimum Temperature +1C/33F

Remarks: Honey Crisp are big sellers, customers really take a shine to this variety after their first taste. Sampling is critical to develop new sales. They can be left out on display for 3-4 days with little impact. Good quality fruit should be firm and have a minimum of 50-70% red color. Canada produces the best quality.

Displaying: Prone to bitter pit, be sure to remove apples showing signs of this disorder. Red side should face up to maximize eye appeal and turn apples sideways to prevent stem punctures. Displaying apples under hot light fixtures can turn them waxy and sales will drop off. Cull soft, waxy and bruised fruit. Bag up and sell at a discount or use for samples. Throw out decayed fruit.

Receiving: If available, check the Lot Number, Grower Number and Packing Date on the boxes. Open boxes and inspect the fruit. Stems should be green or brown, not black or shrivelled. Watch out for cracks around the stem bowl. Look for bruises, bitter pit, decay and mold. Firmly press your thumb against the surface for excessive softness. Reject soft apples and shipments in general with an accumulation of more than 10% defects.

Apples Jonagold

Grades: Ex-Fancy | No.1 | Fancy | Commercial | Orchard Run
Sizes: 36 | 48 | 56 | 64 | 72 | 80 | 88 | 100 | 113 | 125 | 138 | 150+
Cartons: 18kg/40# Standard | 20kg/44# Heavy Pack
Bags: 1.36kg/3# | 2.27kg/5# | 3.64kg/8# | 4.54kg/10#
Bins: 182kg/400# | 364kg/800#
Store: Refrigerated | Optimum Temperature +1C/33F

Remarks: Jonagold sales have lagged as shoppers switch to the honey crisp and pink lady varieties instead. Sampling can improve sales. They can be left out on display for 1-2 days with little impact. Good quality fruit should be firm with a minimum 70% red color or sales will lag. Refrigerate at close for best results. Canada produces the best quality.

Displaying: Prone to bitter pit, be sure to remove apples showing signs of this disorder. Red side should face up to maximize eye appeal and turn apples sideways to prevent stem punctures. Displaying apples under hot light fixtures will turn them waxy and sales will drop off. Cull soft, waxy and bruised fruit. Bag up and sell at a discount or use for samples. Throw out decayed fruit.

Receiving: If available, check the Lot Number, Grower Number and Packing Date on the boxes. Open boxes and inspect the fruit. Stems should be green or brown, not black or shrivelled. Watch out for cracks around the stem bowl. Look for bruises, bitter pit, decay and mold. Firmly press your thumb against the surface for excessive softness. Reject soft apples and shipments in general with an accumulation of more than 10% defects.

Apples McIntosh

Grades: Ex-Fancy | No.1 | Fancy | Commercial | Orchard Run
Sizes: 36 | 48 | 56 | 64 | 72 | 80 | 88 | 100 | 113 | 125 | 138 | 150+
Cartons: 18kg/40# Standard | 20kg/44# Heavy Pack
Bags: 1.36kg/3# | 2.27kg/5# | 3.64kg/8# | 4.54kg/10#
Bins: 182kg/400# | 364kg/800#
Store: Refrigerated | Optimum Temperature +1C/33F

Remarks: "Macs" are an old time favorite and can be left out on display for 1-2 days with little impact. Good quality fruit should be firm with a minimum 50% red color. Quality is mixed even in good years. Refrigerate at close for best results. Developed in the 1820s by John McIntosh, this variety originates in Ontario, Canada.

Displaying: Macs are a soft fleshed variety and bruise easily, handle gently. Red side should face up to maximize eye appeal. Turn apples sideways to prevent stem punctures. Displaying apples under hot light fixtures can turn them waxy and sales will drop off. Sampling can increase sales. Cull soft, waxy and bruised fruit. Bag up and sell at a discount or use for samples. Throw out decayed fruit.

Receiving: If available, check the Lot Number, Grower Number and Packing Date on the boxes. Open boxes and inspect the fruit. Stems should be green or brown, not black or shrivelled. Look for bruises, bitter pit, decay and mold. Firmly press your thumb against the surface for excessive softness. Reject soft apples and shipments in general with an accumulation of more than 10% defects.

Apples Pacific Rose

Grades: Ex-Fancy | No.1 | Fancy | Commercial | Orchard Run
Sizes: 36 | 48 | 56 | 64 | 72 | 80 | 88 | 100 | 113 | 125 | 138 | 150+
Cartons: 18kg/40# Standard | 20kg/44# Heavy Pack
Bags: 1.36kg/3# | 2.27kg/5# | 3.64kg/8# | 4.54kg/10#
Bins: 182kg/400# | 364kg/800#
Store: Refrigerated | Optimum Temperature +1C/33F

Remarks: Pacific Rose (Sciros) are an excellent, flavorful, hard apple. Big sellers and can be left out on display for 3-4 days with little impact. Good quality fruit should be very firm and have a minimum of 50-70% red color. A cross of the Gala and Splendor varieties, New Zealand produces the best quality (exclusively owned and marketed).

Displaying: Very easy to handle, sampling is critical to develop new sales. Red side should face up to maximize eye appeal. Turn apples sideways to prevent stem punctures. Displaying apples under hot light fixtures can turn them waxy and sales will drop off. Cull soft, waxy and bruised fruit. Bag up and sell at a discount or use for samples. Throw out decayed fruit.

Receiving: If available, check the Lot Number, Grower Number and Packing Date on the boxes. Open boxes and inspect the fruit. Stems should be green or brown, not black or shrivelled. Watch out for cracks around the stem bowl. Look for bruises, brown spotting, decay and mold. Firmly press your thumb against the surface for excessive softness. Reject soft apples and shipments in general with an accumulation of more than 10% defects.

43

Apples Pink Lady

Grades: Ex-Fancy | No.1 | Fancy | Commercial | Orchard Run
Sizes: 36 | 48 | 56 | 64 | 72 | 80 | 88 | 100 | 113 | 125 | 138 | 150+
Cartons: 18kg/40# Standard | 20kg/44# Heavy Pack
Bags: 1.36kg/3# | 2.27kg/5# | 3.64kg/8# | 4.54kg/10#
Bins: 182kg/400# | 364kg/800#
Store: Refrigerated | Optimum Temperature +1C/33F

Remarks: Pink Lady aka Cripps Pink are generally marketed poorly in North America. Women love this super hard variety. Sampling is critical to develop new sales. They can be left out on display for 3-4 days with little impact. Good quality fruit should be very firm and have a minimum of 50-70% pink blush or else sales will lag. Native to Australia, all growing regions can produce excellent quality.

Displaying: Very easy to handle. Pink side should face up to maximize eye appeal. Turn apples sideways to prevent stem punctures. Displaying apples under hot light fixtures can turn them waxy and sales will drop off. Cull soft, waxy and bruised fruit. Bag up and sell at a discount or use for samples. Throw out decayed fruit.

Receiving: If available, check the Lot Number, Grower Number and Packing Date on the boxes. Open boxes and inspect the fruit. Stems should be green or brown, not black or shrivelled. Watch out for cracks around the stem bowl. Look for bruises, brown spotting, decay and mold. Firmly press your thumb against the surface for excessive softness. Reject soft apples and shipments in general with an accumulation of more than 10% defects.

Apples Red Delicious

Grades: Ex-Fancy | No.1 | Fancy | Commercial | Orchard Run
Sizes: 36 | 48 | 56 | 64 | 72 | 80 | 88 | 100 | 113 | 125 | 138 | 150+
Cartons: 18kg/40# Standard | 20kg/44# Heavy Pack
Bags: 1.36kg/3# | 2.27kg/5# | 3.64kg/8# | 4.54kg/10#
Bins: 182kg/400# | 364kg/800#
Store: Refrigerated | Optimum Temperature +1C/33F

Remarks: Sales have stagnated during the last decade as shoppers have switched to newer varieties. They can be left out on display for 1-2 days with little impact. Prone to bitter pit, good quality fruit should be very firm. Washington State produces the best quality.

Displaying: Red Delicious are easy to handle however they can turn soft, waxy and pithy quickly. Slow movers, minimize displays at all times. Turn apples sideways to prevent stem punctures. Displaying apples under hot light fixtures can turn them waxy and sales will drop off. Sampling does not improve sales. Cull soft, waxy and bruised fruit. Bag up and sell at a discount or use for samples. Throw out decayed fruit.

Receiving: If available, check the Lot Number, Grower Number and Packing Date on the boxes. Open boxes and inspect the fruit. Stems should be green or brown, not black or shrivelled. Watch out for cracks around the stem bowl. Look for bruises, bitter pit, decay and mold. Firmly press your thumb against the surface for excessive softness. Reject soft apples and shipments in general with an accumulation of more than 10% defects.

Apples Royal Gala

Grades: Ex-Fancy | No.1 | Fancy | Commercial | Orchard Run
Sizes: 36 | 48 | 56 | 64 | 72 | 80 | 88 | 100 | 113 | 125 | 138 | 150+
Cartons: 18kg/40# Standard | 20kg/44# Heavy Pack
Bags: 1.36kg/3# | 2.27kg/5# | 3.64kg/8# | 4.54kg/10#
Bins: 182kg/400# | 364kg/800#
Store: Refrigerated | Optimum Temperature +1C/33F

Remarks: Galas may be the best selling apples in the world and can be left out on display for 2-3 days with little impact. Many "gala" varieties are marketed and sold under the "royal gala" name. Good quality fruit should be very firm and have a minimum of 60-80% red color. All growing regions can produce excellent quality.

Displaying: Easy to handle. Red side should face up to maximize eye appeal. Turn apples sideways to prevent stem punctures. Displaying apples under hot light fixtures can turn them waxy and sales will drop off. Sampling can increase sales by +50%. Cull soft, waxy and bruised fruit. Bag up and sell at a discount or use for samples. Throw out decayed fruit.

Receiving: If available, check the Lot Number, Grower Number and Packing Date on the boxes. Open boxes and inspect the fruit. Stems should be green or brown, not black or shrivelled. Inspect for stemless and cracks around the stem bowl. Look for bruises, bitter pit, decay and mold. Firmly press your thumb against the surface for excessive softness. Reject soft apples and shipments in general with an accumulation of more than 10% defects.

Apples Spartan

Grades: Ex-Fancy|No.1|Fancy|Commercial|Orchard Run
Sizes: 36|48|56|64|72|80|88|100|113|125|138|150+
Cartons: 18kg/40# Standard|20kg/44# Heavy Pack
Bags: 1.36kg/3#|2.27kg/5#|3.64kg/8#|4.54kg/10#
Bins: 182kg/400#|364kg/800#
Store: Refrigerated|Optimum Temperature +1C/33F

Remarks: Spartan are very similar to the McIntosh variety except firmer. They can be left out on display for 2-3 days with little impact. Good quality fruit should be firm with a minimum 50-70% red color. Spartan were developed by Dr. R.C. Palmer in Summerland, B.C. in the1930s.

Displaying: Spartan are a soft fleshed variety and bruise easily, handle gently. Red side should face up to maximize eye appeal. Turn apples sideways to prevent stem punctures. Displaying apples under hot light fixtures can turn them waxy and sales will drop off. Sampling does not improve sales. Cull soft, waxy and bruised fruit. Bag up and sell at a discount or use for samples. Throw out decayed fruit.

Receiving: If available, check the Lot Number, Grower Number and Packing Date on the boxes. Open boxes and inspect the fruit. Stems should be green or brown, not black or shrivelled. Look for bruises, bitter pit, decay and mold. Firmly press your thumb against the surface for excessive softness. Reject soft apples and shipments in general with an accumulation of more than 10% defects.

Apple Pears

Grades: No.1 | Orchard Run
Packs: Single Layer | Tray Pack | Foam | Paper | Bulk
Cartons: 4kg/8.8# | 8kg/17.6# | 10kg/22# | 18kg/40#
Bags(In Cups): 1.36kg/3# | 2.27kg/5#
Bins: 182kg/400#
Store: Refrigerated | Optimum Temperature +1C/33F

Remarks: There are "light" and "dark" skinned varieties of apple pears. Light varieties have more flavor and a thinner skin; dark varieties are generally less desirable, but hold up much better on display. They break down quickly once their protective wrapping is removed; which serves the dual purpose of preventing the skins from discoloring and rubbing against each other.

Displaying: Always dummy displays, shrink will be brutal otherwise. The protective wrapping should only be removed from the top layers or displayed single layer in trays (dummied underneath). Handle gently and turn fruit sideways to prevent stem punctures. Sampling will increase sales. Cull soft, bruised fruit, bag up and sell at a discount or use for samples. Throw out decayed fruit.

Receiving: If available, check the Lot Number, Grower Number and Packing Date on the boxes. Open boxes and inspect the fruit. Stems should be green or brown, not black or shrivelled. Look for bruises, decay and mold. Firmly press your thumb against the surface for excessive softness. Reject soft fruit and shipments in general with an accumulation of more than 10% defects.

Stonefruit Overview

Apricots | Nectarines | Peaches | Plums

"Stonefruit" aka "Treefruit" is usually picked a little bit immature to ensure supermarkets have ample time to sell the fruit (shrink would be unmanageable if all fruit was picked ripe). Volume-fill (VF) cartons are more economical and are generally picked less ripe than Tray-packed aka Panta Pack fruit (TP/PP).

Stonefruit is all about the right varieties and ensuring the fruit you are receiving is from reputable growers. There are a lot of second-rate growers out there that market their fruit strictly on price. In reality you are usually not saving a cent, these growers do a bad job of packing and allow a high percentage of poor quality fruit into their boxes.

Most Purchasing today has been taken away from the warehouse level and moved to a Central Purchasing office. Often it is no longer convenient for Produce Buyers to see first-hand what is being received, they rely on QC (Quality Control) personnel at the warehouse to advise them of any quality issues.

Fruit packed within Grade Specifications cannot usually be rejected for low color, low brix (sugar), no flavor, or for split stones. However, supermarkets can choose to find a better grower/packer to purchase their fruit.

Lousy fruit means more work for you, more culling, more waste and having to listen to shopper's complaints.

The Purchaser should be advised of these issues by someone in authority at Store Level. Photos can help make your case.

Tray-packs are more expensive and normally sold as an alternative to VF cartons. Usually marketed as "tree-ripened" which offers shoppers a "ready to eat" piece of fruit for a premium price. A great alternative for specialty stores that charge high prices, if you do not have time to maintain VF displays; or for supermarkets that want to offer shoppers a choice and list both.

Yellow-fleshed peaches and nectarines emit a wonderful aroma as they ripen, hold the fruit up to your nose and inhale. This useful tidbit of information will endear you to your customers. Unripe fruit has no smell.

White-fleshed peaches do not smell at all, many varieties are grown for their appearance and have almost no flavor or sugar. Learning to carry the right varieties is important, buyers of white-fleshed fruit are very finicky, store returns can be common and you can forget repeat business. Asians prefer to eat these super hard like apples, while Caucasians like to eat them ripe like regular peaches and nectarines.

Apricots and plums do not smell either as they ripen. Apricots turn a golden-yellow/golden-orange when they are ripe; fruit with a greenish tinge or green shoulders will not ripen and only gets soft and mushy.

It is more difficult to assess the ripeness of plums because some varieties are ripe when they are soft and others while still hard. Learning the different aspects of each variety is easy… just take a bite. Sampling fruit is an important part of the learning process.

Split Stone (Pit)

Fruit with split stones should be rejected. The first type is easy to spot...there will be a large "black hole" at the base of the stem. Earwigs (insects) love to crawl inside, if disturbed they have large pinchers that can inflict painful bites. Biting into the affected fruit and having a giant black bug emerge can also cause hysteria.

The second type of split stone can be recognized by its asymmetrical appearance (two sides that don't match). One half of the fruit will have a long "ridge" or "bump" from top to bottom, making the fruit look deformed on one side. There is usually mold inside the core that is noticeable while the fruit is being eaten or the broken pit can become a choking hazard or injure teeth.

Diagram 7A:

Split Stone Should be Rejected

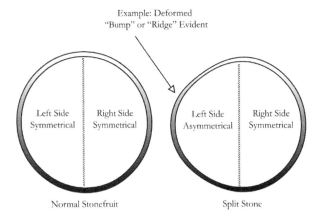

Example: Deformed
"Bump" or "Ridge" Evident

Left Side Symmetrical | Right Side Symmetrical

Left Side Asymmetrical | Right Side Symmetrical

Normal Stonefruit

Split Stone

If you are still unsure, the best test is the taste test. Bite into the fruit and check it out.

Speckled Fruit (dots)

Speckled dots on the bottoms of the Stonefruit is another sure-fire method to tell if the variety you are inspecting is sweet. Another useful tidbit of information you can pass on to your shoppers.

Ripening Fruit

Sometimes your Stonefruit orders will arrive rock hard and green. Sales will slow because shoppers prefer to purchase fruit on the riper side and they worry that the unripe fruit will not ripen up properly and spoil.

You may need to ripen the fruit in the dry-storage area for a couple of days (next to the bananas). Be sure to check it daily and slot into the cooler once the desired ripeness has been achieved.

Sizes

There are too many sizes and packs available globally today to list here. I have included North American guidelines and specs, if you are still unsure ask your supervisor or manager for clarification.

Apricots

Grades: No.1 | No.2 | Orchard Run
Packs: Trays | Bulk | Clamshells | 7L
Sizes: 5 | 6 | 7 | 8 | 10 | 12
Cartons: 4.54kg/10# | 6.36kg/14# | 8.18kg/18# | 10kg/22#
Store: Refrigerated | Optimum Temperature +1C/33F
Stonefruit Overview: Page 49

Remarks: Apricots are one of the most difficult fruit to handle. Always dummy displays to reduce culls and waste. Varieties with red blush taste and sell better.

Displaying: Apricots become soft and quickly deteriorate on display. Stack ripe fruit on top and green fruit on the bottom layers. Put up a sign with the blurb "PLEASE HANDLE GENTLY" to minimize shrink. Sampling can increase sales. Cull soft, overripe fruit, bag up and sell at a discount as "Jam Cots". Do not use overripe fruit for samples, this will slow sales. Throw out decayed fruit.

Receiving: If available, check the Lot Number, Grower Number, Packing Date and Variety on the boxes. Open boxes, fruit should look clean, attractive and be firm to the touch. A small percentage of fruit with a green tinge is to be expected; but remember green fruit will not ripen and is inferior. Branch marks located at the stem bowl are normal as long as the fruit is not damaged or skin broken. Look for bruises, brown spotting, decay and mold. Cut open and inspect around the pit for brown discoloration (a sign of age). Reject soft fruit and shipments in general with an accumulation of more than 10% defects.

Avocados

Grades: Class 1 | 2 | 3
Stages: Firm | Breaking | Ripe
Sizes: 20 | 24 | 28 | 32 | 36 | 40 | 48 | 60 | 70 | 84 | 96
Packs: 1/2/3 Layer | Bags | Bulk
Cartons: 4kg | 6kg/13.2# | 10kg/22# | 11.36kg/25# | 17kg
Store: Unrefrigerated | Optimum Temperature +10C/50F

Remarks: Avocado sales have really taken off in the last few years with supermarkets switching to "pre-ripened" programs to improve sales. "Hass" is the most popular.

Displaying: Easy to handle, ripe fruit should be placed atop displays during peak hours, otherwise keep it cool in the back ripening area. During slow times put up a sign "Ripe Avocados Available Please Ask". This minimizes shrink and allows you to interact with customers. Avocados can be stacked without worry. Cull overripe, black fruit, bag up and discount it, mark "Perfect for Guacamole" on the bags.

Receiving: If available, check the Lot Number, Grower Number, Packing Date and Variety on the boxes. Open boxes, fruit should be clean, firm and without skin defects. Cut open to ensure flesh is not black and been chilled by the truck reefer. Avocados produce a high level of ethylene gas which speeds up ripening. Keep boxes closed to ripen quickly or remove lids (and plastic pallet wrap) to slow down the ripening process. Reject shipments in general with an accumulation of more than 10% defects.

Bananas

Grades: No.1 "Big Bunches" (Hands) | No.2 "Small"
Cartons: 18kg/40# Standard
Bags: 2.27kg/5#
Store: Unrefrigerated | Optimum Temperature +10C/50F

Remarks: Bananas are the most important fruit in the produce department. Relatively inexpensive year-round, everyone can afford to buy and eat bananas. No.1 grade fruit has bigger bunches (called "hands") and is generally more attractive in appearance than No.2 grade. Bigger "hands" means bunches are heavier and therefore less bunches per box; more tonnage is sold and less handling and culling is required.

Displaying: Bananas should not be stacked, this causes significant bruising. Widen displays instead during peak hours to maximize sales. Tiering displays offers a better visual impact. Cull singles, spotted and bruised fruit. Bag up and mark on bags "For Banana Bread" (mark price on bag i.e. $2.00). Ripe bananas for banana bread are always in demand, usually no need to discount.

Receiving: Open boxes and inspect the fruit for brown spotting and bruising. Stage 3-4 is best (turning yellow with green tips), if the tips are yellow the fruit will only last one day before becoming overripe. Green bananas will not ripen. If necessary, remove the plastic pallet wrap and lids to slow down the ripening process (Page 27, Diagram 6B). Reject spotted, bruised and overripe fruit and shipments in general with an accumulation of more than 10% defects.

Blackberries

Grades: No.1/Domestic
Packs: 4.4oz | 6oz | 1 pint | 2 pint | 18oz | 1 quart
Cartons: 1.36kg/3# | 2kg/4.4# | 4kg/8.8# | 4.54kg/10#
Store: Refrigerated | Optimum Temperature +1C/33F

Remarks: Blackberries are picked unripe (small drupelets) to ensure they have a good shelf-life. This has a negative impact on sales, shoppers often complain the berries taste sour. Dummy displays to minimize shrink.

Displaying: If blackberries are attracting fruit flies, place a small portable fan behind the display (the fan will blow them away). Occasionally, when ripe fruit is received it needs to moved quickly. Ripe blackberries will have big drupelets (the sections which make up the berry). Displaying fruit in refrigerated counters is best, although condensation can build up inside the clamshell lid and slow sales. Rotate stock every couple of hours to ensure good movement. Quantity pricing and cross selling with other berry varieties will increase sales.

Receiving: Blackberries are force-air cooled to extend shelf-life, good quality fruit looks bright, fresh and appetizing. Open clamshells and sample, inspect the white pads for purple stains, this is usually an indication of aging fruit. Cases can spoil overnight if mold is found inside the center of just a few berries, this is an indication the fruit was picked after a heavy rainfall (a no-no). Reject dull looking, wet, moldy, or shrivelled fruit and shipments in general with an accumulation of more than 10% defects.

Blueberries

Grades: No.1 | Domestic
Packs: 4.4oz | 6oz | 1 pint | 2 pint | 18oz | 1 quart
Cases: 2kg | 4kg | | 5# | 10# | clamshells & bulk
Store: Refrigerated | Optimum Temperature +1C/33F

Remarks: Easy to handle, blueberries are a big part of produce sales. They have a natural powder called "bloom" on their skin (just like plums). After harvest, blueberries slowly lose their bloom and begin to look dull. A sign the fruit needs to be moved fairly quickly.

Displaying: Blueberries can be stacked several layers high without impact. Dummying displays during slow times will minimize shrink. Displaying fruit in refrigerated counters is best, although condensation can build up inside the clamshell lid and slow sales. Rotate stock every couple of hours to ensure good movement. Quantity pricing and cross selling with other berry varieties will increase sales. Sample whenever possible.

Receiving: Blueberries are force-air cooled to extend their shelf-life. Good quality fruit will have lots of bloom and look bright, fresh and appetizing. Open the clamshells and sample the fruit to see if it is sweet and firm. Inspect for mold and shrivelling. Reject wet, soft, moldy or shrivelled fruit and shipments in general with an accumulation of more than 10% defects. Late varieties of blueberries are normally sour, unavoidable if you want to have fruit year-round. Fruit stored in front of walk-in cooler fans (unless covered) will become chilled and soft.

Cantaloupe Melons

Grades: Fancy|No.1|No.2|Commercial|Orchard Run
Packs: 6|9|12|15|18|23
Cases: 18kgs/40# **Bins:** 182kg/400#|364kg/800#
Store: Refrigerated|Optimum Temperature +1C/33F

Remarks: Easy to handle, cantaloupe (musk melon) should be pulled down at night and put back in the cooler. Overripe fruit can be sold as ½'s, used for fruit salad and samples; throw out as a last resort.

Displaying: Ripe fruit turns golden-yellow and smells wonderful, place atop your displays. Cantaloupe picked "full-slip" (at maturity) have a clean belly-button and will always ripen. Signs of ripped vines on the belly-button means the fruit was picked too early and will not ripen. Dummy displays during slow times to minimize culls.

Receiving: Unscrupulous shippers routinely ship underweight boxes of cantaloupe (industry standard 38-40lbs). Expect boxes to weigh as little as 28lbs. Stores retailing by the pound should always weigh boxes. Your store may be losing substantial money. Report grossly underweight labels to the Purchaser. Open boxes and inspect for bruising (indentations), mold and wet black belly buttons. Fruit packed in plastic liners can arrive wet, inspect closely (later open the plastic liners to allow fruit to dry out). Cantaloupe should be firm, clean and look healthy. If the fruit is ripe (Page 27, Diagram 6B), remove plastic pallet wrap to slow the ripening process. Reject shipments in general with an accumulation of more than 10% defects.

Cherimoya

Grades: No U.S. or International
Packs: Single-Layer/Foam Sleeve/Paper Wrapper
Weights: Sold by Count | 4kg/8.8# | 8kg/17#
Store: Unrefrigerated | Optimum Temperature +10C/50F

Remarks: Cherimoya aka Custard Apple are very popular in tropical climates. Do not list unless you have sufficient ethnic shoppers to purchase this fruit (very expensive and shrink can be horrendous). Cherimoya are delicious although the texture may take some getting used to if you have not eaten this fruit before. Their taste could be compared to a green grape, pineapple flavor and there are a few inedible seeds inside.

Displaying: Do not overstock, cherimoya are very fragile, special care must be taken. Display at room-temperature, refrigerating will chill and blacken the fruit like bananas. They turn light green to yellow when ripe and feel similar to a ripe bartlett pear when they are ready to eat. Display single layer in their cups (foam sleeves) to prevent unnecessary bruising and handling. Placing fruit onto a tray and overwrapping using a hot wrap machine is also a good idea. Pull down at close.

Receiving: Do not over order. Fruit should have a slight softness when you press your thumb lightly against the flesh; look bright and robust. A little bit of black spotting is okay as long as it is not due to being chilled by the truck reefer. Pulp the temperature to be sure. Ripe fruit should be rejected if it cannot be sold immediately because it can spoil in a single day.

Cherries Rainier

Grades: No.1 | No.2 | Domestic | Orchard Run
Sizes: 8 | 8.5 | 9 | 9.5 | 10 | 10.5 | 11 | 11.5 | 12
Cartons: 2kg/4.4# | 5kg/11# | 6.82kg/15# | 9kg/20#
Bags: Random Weight | 1# | 1.5# | 2# | 1kg/2.2#
Clamshells: 1# | 2# | 1.82kg/4#
Store: Refrigerated | Optimum Temperature +1C/33F

Remarks: Rainier cherries are incredibly sweet and delicious; a small rainier display should always complement a red cherry display.

Displaying: Retailing clamshells minimizes shrink, they can be stacked several layers high without impact (dummy displays during slow times). Displaying fruit in refrigerated counters helps too, although condensation can build up inside the container and slow sales. Bagged fruit should be displayed single layer only, widen out displays during peak hours to maximize sales. Offering samples is expensive. Beat up, poor looking fruit should be discounted and sold quickly. Cull bad cherries from bags and clamshells and throw them out.

Receiving: If available, check the Lot Number, Grower Number and Packing Date on the boxes. Look for green stems (attached), firmness and a nice red blush. Dry, brown or loose stems are signs of old or mature fruit. Condensation means the fruit is not fresh or been sitting out. Do not store cherries in front of walk-in cooler fans or they will become chilled and soft. Reject fruit in general with an accumulation of more than 10% defects.

Cherries Red

Grades: No.1 | No.2 | Domestic | Orchard Run
Sizes: 8 | 8.5 | 9 | 9.5 | 10 | 10.5 | 11 | 11.5 | 12
Cartons: 2.5kg/5.5# | 5kg/11# | 9kg/20#
Bags: Random Weight | 1# | 1.5# | 2# | 1kg/2.2#
Clamshells: 1# | 2# | 1.82kg/4#
Store: Refrigerated | Optimum Temperature +1C/33F

Remarks: During summer months cherries are a big part of your sales. Highly perishable, it is important that proper rotation is always followed.

Displaying: Retailing clamshells minimizes shrink, they can be stacked several layers high without impact (dummy displays during slow times). Displaying fruit in refrigerated counters helps too, although condensation can build up inside the container and slow sales. Bagged fruit should be stacked no more than two layers high, widen out displays instead during peak hours to maximize sales. Offering samples is expensive. Beat up, poor looking fruit should be discounted and sold quickly. Cull bad cherries from bags and clamshells and throw them out.

Receiving: If available, check the Lot and Grower Number and Packing Date on the boxes. Fruit should be firm, have green stems (dry, brown or loose stems are signs of age) and a nice sheen. Inspect for splits, cracks, mold and brown rot. Condensation means the fruit is not fresh or been sitting out. Cherries stored in front of walk-in cooler fans can become chilled and soft. Reject cherries with an accumulation of more than 10% defects.

Chestnuts Fresh

Grades: Grade A | Grade B | Fancy | Extra Fancy
Sizes: Small | Standard | Lge | Xlge | Special | Jbo | Giant | Col.
Sizes count per kg: 20-40 | 40-60 | 60-80 | 80-100 | 100-120
Sizes inch: +1.0" | +1.125" | +1.25" | +1.375"
Bags: 5kg/11# | 11.36kg/25# | 20kg/44#
Store: Refrigerated | Optimum Temperature +1C/33F

Remarks: Chestnut quality, grades, size specifications and tastes vary significantly. There are no set industry standards in the USA, growers regulate themselves. To be considered good eating...the shell and inner-skin must peel away easily from the nut (a big complaint among connoisseurs). Italy produces the best quality and California is good too. Korean chestnuts are considered the worst because their inner skin sticks to the nut after being prepared. Chinese product is usually cheaper, quality can be excellent, while other times it's terrible.

Displaying: Easy to handle, chestnuts are widely eaten by ethnic groups that are price sensitive. Heap displays during the holidays with little impact. If your retail is over $4.00/lb, keep displays dummied. Big chestnuts sell much better.

Receiving: Weigh bags and inspect for worm holes, cracks and mold (dull looking product is a sign of age). Chestnuts are usually polished before leaving the farm. They should look bright, shiny and feel heavy in the palm of your hand. If unsure, use the water test... bad chestnuts will float in a sink of water.

Coconuts

Grades: Grade A | Grade B | No.1 | No.2
Bags: 25ct | 40ct | 50ct
Store: Optimum Temperature +1C/33F to +10C/50F

Remarks: : Coconut quality, grades and size specs vary significantly. There are no industry standards in the U.S. Sales have remained unchanged for decades, used as more of a table-filler. "Young" Coconuts however have become popular in large part due to tourism and visits to tropical and sub-tropical climates.

Displaying: Easy to handle, coconuts are price sensitive and an important staple (mainly processed) of many ethnic groups. Displays should be dummied and kept in a secondary location. Quantity pricing is an ideal method to maintain steady sales and keep this product moving.

Receiving: If only all produce was as easy to inspect as coconuts. Open cartons or sacks and shake the coconuts to ensure they are full of juice (reject dry coconuts). Check for cracks and mold, good fruit should be solid and unblemished. Do not drop cartons/sacks or you will crack open the fruit. Coconuts can be stored at room temperature for weeks (refrigerated is better).

Young Coconuts: The giant outer green husk is trimmed down before packing and shipping, making it easier to open and drink the delicious and refreshing nectar inside. Bad product looks dried out with green mold and red-black discoloring and should be rejected.

Dates Medjool Fresh

Grades: Jumbo | Large | Extra Fancy | Fancy | Choice | Cooking
Cartons: 5kg/11# Dried | 11.36kg/25# Fresh
Packaged Dried: 200g | 500g | 1kg | 2kg
Store: Refrigerated | Optimum Temperature +1C/33F

Remarks: It is uncommon to find supermarkets that retail fresh dates in North America. Incredibly sweet and delicious, medjool dates are the most popular variety. Shrink is almost non-existent when marketed correctly.

Displaying: Dates should be sold packaged to eliminate shrink. Using a hot-wrap machine, place dates onto a styrofoam tray and overwrap; or fill clear plastic round tubs with lids. Individually price to avoid problems at the checkout. A mix of ripe and unripe fruit can be combined in the packages, leave the dates attached to their strands with a few loose pieces mixed in. If the dates attract fruit flies, place a small portable fan behind the display (the fan will blow them away). Fresh dates taste so much better than dried, sampling ripe pieces (cut, not whole) is an excellent idea. Refrigerate at close.

Receiving: Fruit should be clean and free of defects. Weigh the boxes, underweight boxes will significantly reduce profits. Fresh dates should be received firm and light brown (tan color) since they will only take a few days to ripen at room temperature on display. Fruit should be attached to their strands. A small percentage of loose and ripe fruit is to be expected, reject shipments in general with an accumulation of more than 20% defects.

Dragon Fruit

Grades: Extra Class | Class 1 | Class 2
Cartons: 4.54kg/10# | 10kg/22# | 25kg/55#
Sizes: 200g | 300g | 400g | 500g | 600g | 700g
Counts: 10 | 12 | 14 | 15 | 16 | 18 | 20+
Store: Refrigerated | Optimum Temperature +1C/33F

Remarks: Dragon fruit adds color and an exotic spice to any produce department. The fruit is sweet when served ripe, but has a very bland flavor. Perfect for fruit plates and garnishes when your customers are looking for something unique. Mass production the past few years has made this fruit as affordable as grapes.

Displaying: Dragon fruit are normally shipped in styrofoam or clear plastic sleeves; this prevents their green offshoots from drying out and turning black. A very finicky fruit, it develops moldy spots as it ripens which make their appearance very ugly; dummy displays to minimize shrink. The flesh turns a translucent greyish color when ripe. Sampling may slow sales. Cull moldy, blackening, wrinkled fruit, bag up and discount or throw out as required.

Receiving: Fruit should be firm, a vibrant pink color and free of defects. Wrinkled green shoots and moldy spots are signs of age. Check stem bowls for insect infestation. Condensation in the plastic sleeves is an indication of age or sitting out too long at room temperature, pulp temperature the flesh. Fruit deteriorates quickly, reject fruit showing these symptoms (mold, wrinkling or softness).

Figs Fresh

Grades: No U.S. or International
Packs: ½ trays | full trays | one pint
Counts: ½ trays 12 | 14 | 16 | 18 | 20
Counts: full trays 20 | 28 | 35 | 40 | 48 | 54
Varieties: Black Mission | Green Calmyrna
Green Kadota | Brown Turkey
Store: Refrigerated | Optimum Temperature +1C/33F

Remarks: Figs do not ripen after being harvested. Ripe fruit will excrete sweet syrup from their openings. During fig season sales can be substantial, but so are the losses. Sales do not usually compensate your losses.

Displaying: Dummy displays. Ethnic groups that love figs prefer to purchase this fruit by the case (these groups are very price conscious). Put a case price on your signage. Sorting through cases to choose the best fruit (causing damage) is common, trays should be overwrapped to prevent severe losses. For shoppers who do not want to purchase cases, offer one pint clamshells. Cull moldy fruit, package and discount.

Receiving: Figs have a very short shelf-life once put up on display, unripe fruit will not sell (hard and firm). Place the fruit between your thumb and index finger and give it a gentle squeeze, it should be slightly soft like a ripe plum. Skin cracks, mold and wrinkling are signs of overripe fruit. However, you must use your discretion when receiving figs and tolerate some defects or no one will ship you any fruit. Reject fruit with more than 20% combined defects.

Grapefruit

Grades: Fancy | Choice
Sizes: 18 | 23 | 27 | 32 | 36 | 40 | 48 | 56
Cartons: 4.54kg/10# | 9kg/20# | 15kg/33# | 18kg/40#
Bags: 1.36kg/3# | 2.27kg/5# | 3.64kg/8# | 4.54kg/10#
Bins: 182kg/400# | 364kg/800#
Store: Refrigerated | Optimum Temperature +1C/33F

Remarks: Easy to handle, carry Texas & Florida grown to avoid sluggish sales, both have excellent quality. Rio Star is the best variety.

Displaying: Grapefruit can be heaped with little impact, small sizes (48/56) sell better bagged, while larger fruit (23/27/32) should be sold by the each or pound. Fruit should be displayed with their bottoms face up for better eye appeal and rotated at least once daily. Sample juicy, sweet varieties to maintain and increase sales.

Receiving: If available, check the Lot Number, Grower Number and Packing Date on the boxes. Open boxes and inspect for mold, decay and softness. Flip boxes upside down, remove bottoms and inspect bottom layers too. If you are in a hurry, use your nose and try to locate a strong citric acid odor, this is an indicator of mold and decay. Weigh boxes, there can be significant weight discrepancies and you may be losing money without even realizing it. A typical 38-40lb box can weigh as little as 23lbs. California grown grapefruit is usually very light (buyer beware). Reject severely underweight shipments and in general with an accumulation of more than 10% defects.

Grapes Overview

Grades: Extra Fancy | Fancy | No.1 Table | No.1 Institutional
Sizes: Small | Medium | Large | Extra Large | Jumbo
Weights: 4.54kg/10# | 8.18kg/18# | 19# | 21# | 22#
Cartons: plastic | styrofoam | wood | cardboard
Packs: Bags 2#/Random Wt. | Clamshells 1#/2#/3#/4#
Store: Refrigerated | Optimum Temperature +1C/33F

Grapes are a big part of produce sales and handling can be very time consuming when facing quality issues.

Diagram 8A:

Use Scissors to trim away bad grapes and stems

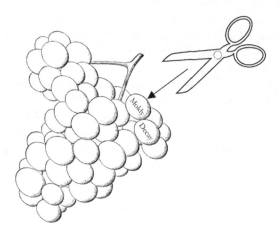

Most supermarkets today purchase bagged grapes and clamshells to keep shrink and labor low. Stack bags no more than two layers high to avoid crushing, try widening displays instead during busy times. Clamshells can be stacked much higher with little impact.

Bloom

Grapes have a natural white powder on their skin called "bloom" (just like plums and blueberries), after packing they lose their bloom as fruit ages and begins to break down. Best quality grapes are usually packed loose and shipped in styrofoam containers.

Trimming

Always keep a small pair of scissors handy. Shoppers love to sample grapes for sweetness before purchasing (it is common to see signs that grapes have been pulled from their bunches or a bad grape or two in the bags). Using your fingers to remove bad grapes can get messy and leave sticky fingerprints on the bags, use a pair of small scissors instead. Trim any signs that the bunches have been disturbed or the fruit may end up sitting on display all day and create more work for you later on.

Shatter

"Shatter" (loose grapes) can be a big problem, especially among the perlette, red crimson and concord grape varieties (these varieties should be sold packaged). Shatter is a good indicator that fruit is getting old, when inspecting orders, gently shake bunches for shatter.

Grapes falling off the vines or excessive loose fruit at the bottom of the containers are bad signs and the shipment should be rejected. Some shatter is unavoidable, use your judgement or ask your supervisor for confirmation.

Popular Varieties

Black Seedless: Fantasy | Summer Royal | Autumn Royal
Black Seeded: Ribier | Concord | Coronation (tiny seed)
Green Seedless: Perlette | Sugarone | Thompson
Green Seeded: Princess | Italia aka Muscat (Muscatel)
Red Seedless: Flame | Crimson | Ruby
Red Seeded: Globe | Red Muscat (becoming popular)

Receiving

If available, check the Lot Number, Grower Number, Packing Date (weigh a couple of boxes too). Inspect grapes for softness, mold, decay, cracks, shatter and wetness. Stems are an good indicator of freshness and often overlooked during inspection, they should be green or brown. Black or brown shrivelled stems means the product is very old. Brown discoloration where the grape attaches to the stem is also a sign of age. Reject shipments in general with an accumulation of more than 10% defects.

Grapes

Grades: Extra Fancy | Fancy | No.1 Table | No.1 Institutional
Sizes: Small | Medium | Large | Extra Large | Jumbo
Weights: 4.54kg/10# | 8.18kg/18# | 19# | 21# | 22#
Packs: Bags 2#/Random Wt. | Clamshells 1#/2#/3#/4#
Store: Refrigerated | Optimum Temperature +1C/33F
Grapes Overview: Page 68

Remarks: Green seedless grape varieties are the most popular, followed by the red and black varieties. Offering samples will increase sales (use "shatter").

Displaying: Rotate grapes regularly as you fill displays to minimize shrink and more work later on. If you are sharing a produce section, ensure your co-workers are stocking in sync with you... front-to-back, back-to-front, etc. (rotating is a waste of time otherwise). Widen displays during busy times, cut back or dummy when slow. Cull cracked, wet, moldy and rotten fruit from displays. Shoppers slipping on grapes and falling on the floor is a rare occurrence, however you must be extra careful when stocking grape displays.

Receiving: If available, check the Lot Number, Grower Number, Packing Date. Weigh boxes. Inspect grapes for softness, mold, decay, cracks, shatter and wetness. Stems are an good indicator of freshness and often overlooked during inspection, they should be green or brown. Black or brown shrivelled stems means the product is very old. Brown discoloration where the grape attaches to the stem is also a sign of age. Reject shipments in general with an accumulation of more than 10% defects.

Grapes for Wine

Many European nationalities purchase wine grapes in the fall to make wine. This can be a profitable category as long as you receive a deposit (50%) or full payment in advance.

Selling wine grapes on spec can be disastrous, thrifty customers will wait until the fruit has been sitting too long and lowball you on prices (you will incur huge losses). At this stage the fruit may even be attracting fruit flies, but this is of little importance to buyers who will be fermenting the grapes anyways.

Normally these shoppers will order multiple lugs (cases) of grapes up to several pallets at one time. Individual purchases can be in the thousands of dollars.

There are many varieties of wine grapes available, another good reason to get advance orders. Lugs of wine grapes look overripe and ugly on arrival, this is because the fruit needs to be harvested at a certain brix (sugar) level or the wine will not be as good. Customers may tell you this is a bad thing in order to negotiate a better price, do not fall for this ploy.

Many customers have switched to purchasing fresh grape juice and forego the process of pressing the grapes themselves. So you may want to offer both to increase sales and keep your regular customers happy.

Investigate and ask lots of questions before offering wine grapes. Regular customers you trust can be a fountain of information.

Honeydew Melons

Grades: No.1 | No.2 | Commercial | Orchard Run
Packs: 4 | 5 | 6 | 7 | 8 | 9 | 10
Cases: 13.64kgs/30# **Bins:** 182kg/400# | 364kg/800#
Store: Refrigerated | Optimum Temperature +1C/33F

Remarks: Easy to handle, it is difficult for shoppers to pick ripe melons; usually they require the expertise of a Produce Clerk. Overripe fruit can be sold as ½'s, used for fruit salad and samples; throw out as a last resort.

Displaying: Ripe honeydew turn a deep yellow hue and/or the rind becomes slightly translucent. Unlike cantaloupe, they do not smell when ripe. The melons will be slightly soft when you press your thumbs against the rind. Honeydew can be heaped with little impact, place ripe fruit on top and dummy displays during slow times. Ripe fruit should be taken down at close and put back in the cooler.

Receiving: A good pack of honeydew weighs 30lbs. Stores retailing by the pound should always weigh the boxes. Your store may be losing substantial money. Report grossly underweight labels to the Purchaser. Open boxes and inspect for brown markings, bruises, mold and decay. Honeydew should be firm, clean and look healthy. Reject ripe fruit if you cannot move it quickly because the flesh can soften and turn mushy within a day on display. If the fruit is ripe (Page 27, Diagram 6B), remove plastic pallet wrap to slow the ripening process. Reject shipments in general with an accumulation of more than 10% defects.

Kiwi Fruit

Grades: No.1 | No.2
Single Layer: 18 | 22 | 25 | 27 | 30 | 33 | 36 | 39 | 42 | 46
Volume Fill: 36 | 41 | 45 | 49 | 52 | 58 | 64 | 71 | 78
Single Layer Trays: 8# Green | 7.5# Gold
Volume Fill Cases: 9kgs/20# | 10kg/22#
Bags: 2# | 1kg   **Bins:** 57kg/125#
Store: Refrigerated | Optimum Temperature +1C/33F

Remarks: Kiwi fruit are so easy to handle and there are many pack sizes available globally (too many to list here). Kiwi is bought, eaten and enjoyed everywhere.

Displaying: Kiwi can be heaped with little impact (rotate at least once daily). Dummying displays makes rotation much easier, although this is not necessary unless the fruit is ripe. Bags should be stacked no more than two layers high to avoid crushing. Ripe fruit should be taken down at close and put back in the cooler.

Receiving: Usually very easy to handle and receive, kiwi can last up to four weeks in your cooler. However during gaps in harvests, fruit is pulled from storage and you may encounter quality issues. If available, check the Lot Number, Grower Number and Packing Date on the boxes. Open and inspect for soft, wrinkled and moldy fruit (all signs of age). If the fruit is wet, inspect closely for mold. Condensation on the plastic liner is usually a sign the fruit has been sitting out somewhere too long, but is not usually an issue. Reject shipments in general with an accumulation of more than 10% defects.

Lemons

Grades: Fancy | Choice | Standard | Cat 1 | Cat 2
Sizes: 75 | 95 | 115 | 140 | 165 | 200 | 235
Cartons: 4.54kg/10# | 9kg/20# | 15kg/33# | 18kg/40#
Bags: 2# | 1.36kg/3# | 2.27kg/5#
Store: Refrigerated | Optimum Temperature +1C/33F

Remarks: Very easy to handle, lemons are a staple of the produce department. Argentina is the world's biggest producer. China has excellent quality available.

Displaying: Lemons can be heaped with little impact. Sales are consistent, although quantity pricing will increase tonnage significantly. Choice grade should only be offered in-season (not from storage), otherwise Fancy grade should be carried. Rotate at least once daily, cull wrinkled, rusty and soft fruit from display, bag up and sell at a discount. Throw out decayed fruit.

Receiving: If available, check the Lot Number, Grower Number and Packing Date. Open boxes and inspect for softness, wrinkles, rust, rusty tips and mold. Turn boxes over and check for wet bottoms and a strong citrus odor (signs of decay and mold). Reject shipments with green mold (spreads quickly) and shipments in general with an accumulation of more than 10% defects. Cost reflects grade, lower your standards if carrying Choice grade.

Meyer Lemons: You will occasionally be asked for this sweet variety. Much more expensive, not a bad idea to have a tiny display if your store has the clientele.

Limes Persian

Grades: No.1 | No.2 | Combination | Cat 1 | Cat 2
Sizes: 110 | 150 | 175 | 200 | 230 | 250
Cartons: 4.54kg/10# | 17-18kg/38-40#
Key Limes: 1#/2# bags
Store: Refrigerated | Optimum Temperature +1C/33F

Remarks: Easy to handle, Persian are the main variety sold in North American supermarkets. A small bagged key lime display will complement your Persian display.

Displaying: Limes breakdown quickly once put out on display. Dummy displays and rotate fruit a couple of times daily. Quantity pricing is ideal to maintain steady sales and avoid excess culling. Once fruit begins to breakdown and show signs of wrinkling and brown spots, it can be very difficult to sell. Even deep discounting does not always work. Neighborhood bars and restaurants will usually purchase overripe lemons and limes at a discount. Throw out decayed fruit.

Receiving: If available, check the Lot Number, Grower Number and Packing Date. Open boxes and inspect for brown spotting and mold, cut open a couple of limes and check the flesh for dryness. Fruit should look bright, fresh and be free of defects. Brown spotted fruit (even a single spot) will spoil quickly once put up on display and should be rejected. Weigh boxes too, severely underweight boxes can be a sign that the fruit has dried out and is not good to sell. Reject shipments in general with an accumulation of more than 10% defects.

Lychee/Longan

Grades: No U.S. or International
Cartons: 2kg/4.4# | 4.54kg/10# | 6kg/13..2# | 10kg/22#
Store: Refrigerated | Optimum Temperature +1C/33F

Remarks: Lychee and their cousin "Longan" (dragon eyes) are favorites among the Asian peoples. Although they all look the same on the outside, varieties differ by the size of their pits. Cheap varieties are 70-80% pit and contain very little meat; these varieties do not sell well.

Displaying: Difficult to retail, customers usually pull fruit from their branches and leave a big mess. Stemless fruit (no branches) can be purchased as an alternative at a slightly higher cost. Shoppers will sample fruit with or without your permission and discard the pits and shells on the floor and display; leave a small waste basket beside the display to make disposal and clean-up easier. Fruit should be retailed in clamshells or bunched up with elastic bands in vexar bags. Lychee dry out quickly, rotate displays regularly and keep a water spray bottle handy to wet the fruit regularly and extend shelf-life.

Receiving: Check the lot number on the boxes. Open and inspect for mold, softness, cracked shells, brown discoloration and pit size (sample). Lychee should be firm. Fruit with red blush sells better. Branches (green leaves) should be brown and fresh looking, not dried out. Wet fruit can turn moldy quickly (wet throughout box) and should be sold within two days. Reject shipments in general with an accumulation of more than 10% defects.

Mango

Grades: Fancy | No.1 | No.2
Sizes: 5 | 6 | 7 | 8 | 9 | 10 | 12 | 14 | 16
Cartons: 2kg/4.4# | 4kg/8.8#
Varieties: Haden | Kent | Keitt | Tommy Atkins
Store: Unrefrigerated | Optimum Temperature +10C/50F

Remarks: Mangos popularity may only be surpassed by bananas. Fruit sells better with red blush and on the riper side. Mango emit a wonderful aroma when ripe.

Displaying: Ripe fruit and fruit with red blush should be displayed on top. Greenish mangos do not sell well, although the Keitt and Kent varieties are both excellent and not stringy. Haden sell best and turn a beautiful red-yellow color when ripe, but have stringy flesh. Tommy Atkins are strictly bred for color, they look beautiful and fill-in gaps between the better varieties. Tommys are a terrible variety, too stringy and tough. Green unripe fruit can be kept in a warm back storage area to ripen further before being put up on display. Cull spotted and overripe fruit, bag up and discount or sample.

Receiving: Check the lot number and variety. Open and inspect for black spots, mold and overripe fruit. Push on stem tops to ensure the flesh is not rotten. Ripe fruit smells, unripe fruit does not. Cut open and inspect flesh for signs of chilling (black discoloration). If the fruit is ripe, remove pallet wrap to slow the ripening process; otherwise leave it on (lids closed) and store in a warm area. Reject shipments in general with an accumulation of more than 10% defects.

Mango Yellow

Grades: Fancy | No.1 | No.2 **Sizes:** 10 | 12 | 14 | 16 | 18 | 20
Cartons: 2kg/4.4# | 4kg/8.8#
Varieties: Ataulfo | Alphonso
Store: Unrefrigerated | Optimum Temperature +10C/50F

Remarks: Yellow mango sales have steadily increased as Caucasian shoppers discover this wonderful fruit. A favorite among Asians, Ataulfo may occasionally outsell your regular varieties. Yellow mangos do not smell.

Displaying: Ripe fruit (deep yellow color) should be displayed on top. Greenish mangos do not sell well, leave them in a warm back storage area to ripen and color up. The Ataulfo variety is excellent and has very few fibers, while the Alphonso is very stringy like the Tommy Atkins. I do not recommend carrying the Alphonso variety ever. Cull spotted, wrinkled and overripe fruit, bag up and discount or sample. Sampling can increase sales +100%.

Receiving: Check the lot number and variety. Open and inspect for black spots, wrinkles, mold and overripe fruit. Spotted fruit will turn quickly and solid green fruit will not ripen properly. Push on stem tops to ensure the flesh is not rotten. Pale dull looking fruit can be a sign of chilling. Cut open and inspect flesh for signs of chilling (black discoloration), common for these two varieties. Sample. If the fruit is ripe, remove pallet wrap to slow the ripening process; otherwise leave it on (lids closed) and store in a warm area. Reject shipments in general with an accumulation of more than 10% defects.

Melons Specialty

Grades: Fancy | No.1 | No.2 | Orchard Run
Packs: 4 | 5 | 6 | 7 | 8 | 9 | 10
Cases: 13.64kg/30#   **Bins:** 400# | 800#
Varieties: Crenshaw | Santa Claus | Canary | Persian | Galia
Store: Refrigerated | Optimum Temperature +1C/33F

Remarks: Specialty melons are a high shrink category, expensive and often more trouble than they are worth. Many new varieties have been introduced in the last few years as global markets open up. The problem with relatively unknown new varieties is, they are usually more expensive, sit around and eventually get thrown out. Due to their size, expensive to sample too.

Displaying: Specialty melons are normally shipped very firm and often they soften and rot in their centers before they ripen (Galia especially). If possible, pull down displays at close (ripe fruit should be pulled down at night and put back in the cooler). Dummy displays to minimize losses. Retailing beside cantaloupe and honeydew is always a good idea. Overripe fruit can be sold as ½'s, used for fruit salad and samples; throw out as a last resort.

Receiving: Weigh boxes, report grossly underweight labels to the Purchaser. Open boxes and inspect for overripe, soft, mold and wet black belly buttons. Sample if unsure. Melons should be firm, clean and look healthy. If the fruit is ripe (Page 27, Diagram 6B), remove plastic pallet wrap to slow ripening. Reject shipments in general with an accumulation of more than 10% defects.

Nectarines Red

Grades: No.1 | No.2 (Utility) | Orchard Run
Trays: 30/36 | 40/44 | 48/50 | 54/56 | 60/64 | 70/72 | 80+
Bulk: 30/34 | 36 | 40 | 42 | 44 | 48 | 50 | 56 | 60 | 64 | 70 | 72 | 80+
Cartons: 4.54kg/10# | 8.18kg/18# | 10kg/22# | 11.36kg/25#
Store: Refrigerated | Optimum Temperature +1C/33F
Stonefruit Overview: Page 49

Remarks: Easy to handle. Ripe fruit should be pulled down at close. Varieties with round bottoms (not pointy) hold up better and are much sweeter.

Displaying: Firm nectarines can be left on display for 1-2 days with little impact. Ripe fruit emits a wonderful aroma, stack on top to move quickly. Display red side face up to maximize eye appeal. Put up a sign "Please Handle Gently" to minimize shrink. Rotate regularly but always keep ripe fruit on top. Sampling can increase sales. Cull soft, overripe fruit, bag up and sell at a discount. Do not use overripe fruit for samples, this will deter sales. Throw out decayed fruit. Cross-selling with peaches and other stone fruit works great and moves extra tonnage.

Receiving: If available, check the Lot Number, Grower Number, Packing Date and Variety. Open boxes and inspect fruit for color (green tinge), cracks and rot. Cut open and inspect for split stone. Sample. Bottoms with a tiny black dot on their tips (needle size) can spoil on display in one day and should be rejected. Fruit should be clean, attractive and firm to the touch. Reject fruit in general with an accumulation of more than 10% defects.

Nectarines White

Grades: No.1| No.2 (Utility)|Orchard Run
Trays: 30/36|40/44|48/50|54/56|60/64|70/72|80+
Bulk: 30/34|36|40|42|44|48|50|56|60|64|70|72|80+
Cartons: 4.54kg/10#|8.18kg/18#|10kg/22#|11.36kg/25#
Store: Refrigerated|Optimum Temperature +1C/33F
Stonefruit Overview: Page 49

Remarks: Easy to handle, most Asians love to eat these hard like apples. The best varieties have high "brix" (sugar) and taste super sweet while still firm. Varieties with round bottoms (not pointy) hold up better and are much sweeter.

Displaying: Firm nectarines can be left on display for 2-3 days with little impact. Ripe fruit emits a wonderful aroma, stack on top to move quickly. Display red side face up to maximize eye appeal. Put up a sign "Please Handle Gently" to minimize shrink. Rotate regularly and pull down ripe fruit at close. Sampling can increase sales +100%. Cull soft, overripe fruit, bag up and sell at a discount. Do not use overripe fruit for samples, this will deter sales. Throw out decayed fruit.

Receiving: If available, check the Lot Number, Grower Number, Packing Date and Variety. Open boxes and inspect fruit for color (green tinge), cracks and rot. Cut open and inspect for split stone. Sample. Bottoms with a tiny black dot on their tips (needle size) can spoil on display in one day and should be rejected. Fruit should be clean, attractive and firm to the touch. Reject fruit in general with an accumulation of more than 10% defects.

Oranges Overview

Navels | Valencia | Mandarins | Tangerines

Oranges, mandarins (seedless) and tangerines (seeded) are available year-round and carrying a good selection is key to healthy sales. Too many varieties will confuse shoppers. Seedless varieties sell best although seeded fruit is a healthier choice. Be sure to sample new varieties. Valencia and Hamlin oranges are juice varieties and do not eat as well as Navels.

Popular Varieties

- Navel oranges (seedless)
- Valencia oranges (seeded)
- Clementine mandarins (seedless)
- Satsuma mandarins (seedless)
- Nan Feng "miniature" mandarins (seedless)
- Christmas mandarins (seedless)
- Honey aka Murcott tangerines (seeded)
- Dancy tangerines (seeded)

Displaying

Oranges can be heaped and left out on display for 2-3 days with little impact. Using the blurbs "seedless" and "super sweet" on your signage will increase sales. These are an ideal table filler when you have extra space available and bin displays work well too (sales can increase by 200-300%).

Valencia oranges go through a process call re-greening, which occurs after the fruit has been harvested (they turn from orange back to green). Very unattractive and shoppers believe green oranges are sour; not always true but sales will diminish regardless. Keep displays small and inventory light, rotate regularly. Green fruit should be pulled from displays, bagged up and discounted as "juice oranges".

Receiving

Many growers and packers today have implemented North American pack sizes and grades to market their fruit more easily. Although, there are third-world countries that still pack fruit as if it was being trucked to the neighbourhood supermarket instead of 6,000 miles away. Avoid headaches by ensuring fruit has been inspected properly on arrival.

Imported produce is usually shipped by ocean container. After 14-30 days on the water (depending on origin) fruit can dry out, become chilled by the reefer, or begin to mold and spoil. Weigh boxes. Check Lot numbers, Grower Numbers and Packing Dates to ensure they match (otherwise inspect fruit from each lot). A strong citrus smell is usually an indication the fruit has begun to breakdown and green mold has set in.

Customers will look directly into your eyes and ask if the oranges are sweet…some people have the ability to read when a person is lying. Sample the fruit yourself whenever possible so shoppers can see the truth in your eyes.

Oranges Mandarins

Grades: Fancy | Choice | No.1 | Cat 1
Sizes: 40 | 50 | 60 | 70 | 80 | 90 | 100 | 110 | 120
Cartons: 1kg | 2kg | 5# | 8# | 9# | 10# | 11# | 22# | 33# | 38-40#
Bags: 1.36kg/3# | 2.27kg/5#
Popular: Satsuma | Clementine | Nan Feng | Xmas | Kinnow
Store: Refrigerated | Optimum Temperature +1C/33F
Oranges Overview: Page 83

Remarks: Mandarins are seedless or "almost" seedless. Although the terms "mandarin" and "tangerine" are loosely interchanged, tangerines are seeded. A big part of seasonal sales, Christmas mandarins boost sales.

Displaying: Mandarins will dry out within a couple of days on display because of their thinner skin. Using the blurb "easy-to-peel" on your signage will increase sales. Displays can be heaped with little impact, but dummy if you are also offering bags or boxes for sale. Additional blurbs like "save buy the bag", "save buy the box" or "save $1.25 buy the box" will increase sales too. Offer samples. Cull soft, wrinkled, spotted and green fruit, bag up and discount. Throw out decayed fruit.

Receiving: If available, check the Lot Number, Grower Number and Packing Date. Open and inspect fruit for softness, cracks, brown spotting, mold, decay and green color. Fruit should be clean, attractive, firm and have green stems. Dull looking fruit is a sign of age. Weigh boxes and sample. Reject fruit in general with an accumulation of more than 10% defects.

Oranges Navels

Grades: Fancy | Choice | No.1 | Cat 1
Sizes: 32 | 36 | 48 | 56 | 64 | 72 | 80 | 88 | 100 | 113 | 125+
Cartons: 4.54kg/10# | 6.36kg/14# | 10kg/22# | 33# | 38-40#
Bags: 1.36kg/3# | 2.27kg/5# | 3.64kg/8# | 4.54kg/10#
Bins: 182kg/400# | 364kg/800#
Store: Refrigerated | Optimum Temperature +1C/33F
Oranges Overview: Page 83

Remarks: Navel oranges are seedless and the most popular variety sold in the world (called "navel" because of their bottom's similarity to a "belly-button").

Displaying: Easy to handle. Displays can be heaped and left out for 2-3 days with little impact. Using the blurbs "easy-to-peel", "seedless" and "super sweet" on your signage (be sure it's true) and offering samples are all great ways to increase sales. Rotate displays regularly. Cull green, soft, wrinkled and spotted fruit, bag up and discount or use for samples. Throw out decayed fruit.

Receiving: If available, check the Lot Number, Grower Number, Packing Date and the bottoms of the boxes for wetness (a sign of decay). Weigh boxes, inspect for softness, brown spotting, mold, decay and green color. Fruit should be clean, attractive, firm and have green stems. Dull looking fruit is a sign of age. Oranges are usually retailed by the pound, be careful of unscrupulous shippers that ship underweight boxes of fruit. Sample for taste, sugar and dryness. Reject fruit in general with an accumulation of more than 10% defects.

Oranges Tangerines

Grades: Fancy | Choice | No.1 | Cat 1
Sizes: 40 | 50 | 60 | 70 | 80 | 90 | 100 | 110 | 120 | 150
Cartons: 5# | 8# | 9# | 10# | 11# | 22# | 33# | 38-40#
Bags: 1.36kg/3# | 2.27kg/5#
Popular: Honey/Murcott | Dancy | Tangelo | Fairchild
Store: Refrigerated | Optimum Temperature +1C/33F
Oranges Overview: Page 83

Remarks: Tangerines contain seeds and are usually juicier and more flavorful than mandarins. Natural varieties of seeded fruit generally have more flavor than their seedless cousins. Showing customers how to easily remove seeds will ensure steady sales and less culling. Visit my website for a short video tutorial on how to easily remove seeds.

Displaying: Tangerines have a good shelf-life (not minneola tangelos) and displays can be heaped with little impact. Using the blurb "easy-to-peel" on your signage will increase sales. Offer samples (remove seeds first). Cull soft, wrinkled and spotted fruit, bag up and discount. Throw out decayed fruit.

Receiving: If available, check the Lot Number, Grower Number and Packing Date. Inspect fruit for softness, cracks, brown spotting, mold and decay. Honey aka Murcott tangerines are waxed to extend their shelf-life. Fruit should be clean, attractive, firm and have green stems. Dullness is a sign of age. Weigh boxes and sample. Reject Tangelos with brown tips and fruit in general with an accumulation of more than 10% defects.

Papaya

Grades: Hawaiian No.1 | No other standard grades
Sizes: 6 | 8 | 10 | 12 | Random
Cartons: 4kg/8.8# | 4.54kg/10# | 11.35kg/25# | 35# | 40#
Store: Unrefrigerated | Optimum Temperature +10C/50F

Remarks: There are two types of papaya available... the Hawaiian pear-shaped type with a typical weight of one pound (yellow-fleshed and premium red-fleshed)...and the larger Caribbean type which weigh as much as twenty pounds (sold green for salads or ripe for eating out of hand). The Hawaiian types are better eating and more expensive because they are "jet-fresh" flown-in by plane.

Displaying: Always dummy displays. The Caribbean variety breaks down much more quickly (even while still green and firm). Papaya should be stacked no more than 2-3 layers high with ripe yellow fruit on top (ripe fruit emits a wonderful aroma). Stem rot is the biggest quality problem, however black mold spots will begin to appear on the fruit too if it is not moved within a few days. Cull soft, overripe and moldy fruit from displays, sell as halves, sample or throw out as necessary.

Receiving: If available, check the Lot Number, Grower Number, Packing Date and weigh boxes. Inspect fruit for stem rot, mold and softness. Fruit should be bright, clean, attractive, and firm. Dull looking fruit is a sign of age. If fruit is ripe, open lids to slow the ripening process (Page 27, Diagram 6B). Reject overripe fruit and fruit in general with an accumulation of more than 10% defects.

Peaches Red

Grades: No.1 | No.2 (Utility) | Orchard Run
Trays: 30/36 | 40/44 | 48/50 | 54/56 | 60/64 | 70/72 | 80/84+
Bulk: 30/34 | 36 | 40 | 42 | 44 | 48 | 50 | 56 | 60 | 64 | 70 | 72 | 80+
Cartons: 4.54kg/10# | 8.18kg/18# | 10kg/22# | 11.36kg/25#
Store: Refrigerated | Optimum Temperature +1C/33F
Stonefruit Overview: Page 49

Remarks: Easy to handle, pull down ripe fruit at close. Fruit with green shoulders will not ripen, varieties with round bottoms hold up better and are much sweeter.

Displaying: Firm peaches can be left on display for 1-2 days with little impact. Ripe fruit emits a wonderful aroma, stack on top to move quickly. Display red side face up to maximize eye appeal. Put up a sign "PLEASE HANDLE GENTLY" to minimize shrink. Rotate regularly but always keep ripe fruit on top. Sampling can increase sales. Cull soft, overripe fruit, bag up and sell at a discount. Do not use overripe fruit for samples, this will deter sales. Throw out decayed fruit. Cross-selling with nectarines and other stone fruit works great and moves extra tonnage.

Receiving: If available, check the Lot Number, Grower Number, Packing Date and Variety. Inspect fruit for color (green tinge), cracks and rot. Cut open and inspect for split stone. Sample. Bottoms with a tiny black dot on their tips (needle size) can spoil on display within a day and should be rejected. Fruit should look clean, attractive and be firm to the touch. Reject fruit in general with an accumulation of more than 10% defects.

Peaches White

Grades: No.1 | No.2 (Utility) | Orchard Run
Trays: 30/36 | 40/44 | 48/50 | 54/56 | 60/64 | 70/72 | 80/84+
Bulk: 30/34 | 36 | 40 | 42 | 44 | 48 | 50 | 56 | 60 | 64 | 70 | 72 | 80+
Cartons: 4.54kg/10# | 8.18kg/18# | 10kg/22# | 11.36kg/25#
Store: Refrigerated | Optimum Temperature +1C/33F
Stonefruit Overview: Page 49

Remarks: Easy to handle, Asians love to eat these hard like apples. The best varieties have high "brix" (sugar) and taste sweet while still firm. Varieties with round bottoms hold up better and are much sweeter.

Displaying: Firm peaches can be left on display for 1-2 days with little impact. Ripe white peaches do not smell, press gently against the flesh to test ripeness. Stack ripe fruit on top to move quickly. Display red side face up to maximize eye appeal. Put up a sign "PLEASE HANDLE GENTLY" to minimize shrink. Rotate regularly and pull down ripe fruit at close. Sampling can increase sales +100%. Cull soft, overripe fruit, bag up and sell at a discount. Do not use overripe fruit for samples, this will deter sales. Throw out decayed fruit.

Receiving: If available, check the Lot Number, Grower Number, Packing Date and Variety. Inspect the fruit for color (green tinge), cracks and rot. Cut open and inspect for split stone. Sample. Bottoms with a tiny black dot on their tips (needle size) can spoil on display in one day and should be rejected. Fruit should look clean, attractive and be firm to the touch. Reject fruit in general with an accumulation of more than 10% defects.

Pears Overview

Easy to handle, Bartlett are the most popular variety. Shoppers easily recognize the bright yellow color of a ripe Bartlett. The Packham tastes almost identical to Bartlett, but their skin is slightly thicker and remains green when ripe. Sales will slow because most shoppers cannot tell when the fruit is ripe. Educating your customers on choosing and ripening pears will ensure steady movement.

<u>Popular Varieties</u>

- Bartlett
- Packham
- Anjou
- Bosc
- Comice
- Seckel
- Concorde
- Forelle

<u>Displaying</u>

During peak season large table and bin displays can be featured, shoppers look forward to in-season promos. Ripe fruit should be placed on top of displays. Stem punctures are common if the fruit is ripe, keep excess ripe fruit in the cooler and replenish as required. Bartlett need to be refrigerated at close. Dummy displays if your inventory is turning quickly and offer ripe samples.

Ripe pears emit a wonderful aroma, but breaking fruit (almost ripe) does not. To determine the ripeness of a pear, hold fruit in the palm of your hand and press your thumb firmly against the flesh. Breaking fruit should feel slightly soft, once this stage is reached the fruit will turn rapidly and should be pulled down at close.

Pears produce a high percentage of ethylene gas which speeds up the ripening process. Shoppers can store fruit in a plastic bag (two is better) at room temperature, this traps the ethylene and induces ripening faster. Once the desired ripeness is achieved the fruit should be removed from the plastic bag and stored in the fridge.

Receiving

Pears are usually packed and shipped individually wrapped to ensure a good arrival. Remove wrappers and inspect a few pieces of fruit. Good quality fruit should be firm to breaking. The overpowering aroma of pears is an indication of overripe fruit. Wet boxes are usually a sign the fruit has begun to breakdown, inspect closely for stem rot, mold and decay. Remove plastic pallet wrap if you need to slow the ripening process (Page 27, Diagram 6B).

Receiving unripe, hard fruit will also slow sales. To speed up the ripening process, pears should be wrapped in plastic pallet wrap and stored in your banana ripening area or at room temperature. Inspect daily for ripeness and move to the cooler once the desired ripeness is reached.

Pears

Grades: Ex-Fancy | Fancy | No.1 | Combo | No.2 | Orch. Run
Sizes: 60 | 70 | 80 | 90 | 100 | 110 | 120 | 135+
Cartons: 4.54kg/10# | 9kg/20# | 18kg/40# | 20kg/44#
Bags: 1.36kg/3# | 2.27kg/5#
Bins: 227kg/500# | 454kg/1000#
Store: Refrigerated | Optimum Temperature +1C/33F
Pears Overview: Page 91

Remarks: Firm pears can be left out on display for 1-3 days with little impact, ripe fruit needs to be put away at close. Sample ripe green varieties to maintain sales and reduce culling. Write blurbs like "I stay green when ripe" or "Ask us how to choose ripe pears" on your signage.

Displaying: Prone to bitter pit (especially Bosc), be sure to remove pears showing signs of this disorder. Ripe fruit should be displayed on top, to prevent stem punctures turn pears sideways. Cull spotted, bruised and overripe fruit, bag up and sell at a discount or use for samples. Throw out moldy and decayed fruit.

Receiving: If available, check the Lot Number, Grower Number and Packing Date. Weigh boxes, open and inspect fruit, stems should be green or brown, not black or shrivelled. Wet wrappings are usually a sign of decay in the box. Check for excessive russeting around the stem, bruising, bitter pit, decay and mold. Firmly press your thumb against the surface to test ripeness. Overripe fruit and shipments in general with an accumulation of more than 10% defects should be rejected.

Persimmons

Grades: In USA graded by color & size | No.1 | No.2
Sizes: 12 | 14 | 16 | 18 | 20 | 22 | 24 | 26 | 28 | 30 | 32+
Cartons: 3kg/6.6# | 4kg/8.8# | 10kg/22# | 11.36kg/25# | 40#
Bags: 1.36kg/3# | 2.27kg/5#   **Bins:** 182kg/400# | 800#
Store: Refrigerated | Optimum Temperature +1C/33F

Remarks: Persimmons cater to a huge ethnic market. The two common varieties are Hachiya (pointy) and Fuyu (flat). Hachiya can only be consumed ripe (very soft) and are widely eaten by Italian and Middle Eastern peoples. Fuyu can be eaten hard like apples or soft like overripe plums and are purchased almost exclusively by Asians. The flavor and textures are completely different between ripe and unripe fruit, almost as if you were looking at two completely different varieties of fruit.

Displaying: Premium single-layer fruit is sold by each, and cheaper volume-fill 25lb boxes by the pound, put a realistic case price on your signage too (case sales are significant). Ripe persimmons do not hold up and need to be sold daily, do not pre-ripen fruit. Dummy displays and place ripe fruit on top. Cull distressed fruit, bag up and discount. Sampling is messy and not recommended. Throw out decayed fruit.

Receiving: If available, check the Lot Number, Grower Number and Packing Date. Weigh boxes. Inspect for green leaves, check for spotting, black discoloration and punctures. Dried out, ugly and overripe fruit and shipments in general with an accumulation of more than 10% defects should be rejected.

Pineapple

Grades: Fancy | No.1 | No.2 | Hawaii Fancy | Hawaii No.1
Single-layer: 4 | 5 | 6 | 7 | 8 | 9 | 10
Two-layer: 8 | 10 | 12 | 14 | 18
Cartons: 9kg/20# | 12kg/26.4# | 18kg/40#
Store: Unrefrigerated | Optimum Temperature +10C/50F

Remarks: Hawaiian pineapple are the best quality, while Mexican is usually the worst because it's picked too green. Pineapple do not ripen after being harvested. Most growers offer a premium grade "ripe-n-ready" pineapple referred to as "gold" or "jet-fresh".

Displaying: Pineapple can be stacked several layers high with little impact. Stack riper fruit on top and rotate regularly. Ripe pineapple emit a wonderful tropical aroma. Cull fruit showing signs of mold, decay or dryness, this includes dried out leaves and moldy bottoms. Overripe fruit can be sold as ½'s, used for fruit salad and samples; throw out as a last resort.

Receiving: If available, check the Lot Number, Grower Number and Packing Date. Weigh boxes, inspect fruit for color, mold and maturity. A green-reddish color on the bottom is a sign of decay beginning to set in. Dry brown leaves and leaves coming away too easily from the fruit are signs of age (test by pulling on leaves). Firmly press your thumbs against the surface for softness. Fruit with a dull translucent appearance is an indicator of chilling. Overripe fruit and shipments in general with an accumulation of more than 10% defects should be rejected.

Plums

Grades: No.1| No.2 (Utility)|Orchard Run
Sizes: 30/35|40/45|50/55|60/65|70|80|90+
Cartons: 4.54kg/10#|8.18kg/18#|12.73kg/28#
Store: Refrigerated|Optimum Temperature +1C/33F
Stonefruit Overview: Page 49

Remarks: Easy to handle, there are so many pack sizes and varieties to choose from. Plumcots and pluots are varieties of "interspecific" plums (plums crossbred with apricots). Plums are very susceptible to mold and need to be rotated regularly; pull down ripe fruit at close.

Displaying: Plums have a natural white powder on their skin called bloom", as plums age they lose their bloom and need to be moved quickly. Firm plums can be left on display for 1-2 days with little impact, stack ripe fruit on top. Sampling can increase sales. Cull soft, overripe fruit, bag up and sell at a discount. Throw out decayed fruit. Cross-selling with other varieties of plums and stone fruit works great and moves extra tonnage.

Receiving: If available, check the Lot Number, Grower Number, Packing Date and Variety. Open boxes and inspect fruit for softness, cracks, scabs and rot. For prune plum types and light fleshed varieties, cut open and check for brown residue around the stone (a sign of age). Sample. Plums should have lots of bloom, look bright, clean, attractive and be firm to the touch. Reject overripe fruit and fruit in general with an accumulation of more than 10% defects.

Pomegranate

Grades: In USA graded by size | Utility
Sizes: 16 | 20 | 24 | 30 | 36 | 42 | 48
Cartons: 5kg/11# | 10kg/22# | Bulk Bins
Store: Refrigerated | Optimum Temperature +5-6C/41-43F

Remarks: Dark red pomegranates like the "Wonderful" variety sell best. Fruit needs to be pulled down at close.

Displaying: Easy to handle. There is a significant price gap between small and large sizes (large fruit sells better). Quantity pricing will help ensure steady movement. Displays should be dummied and rotated regularly to minimize culls. Once this fruit begins to dry out, crack, turn brown and breakdown it's difficult to move. During Thanksgiving and Christmas seasons, pomegranates are often used as holiday centerpieces. Bag up culls and sell at a discount. Throw out decayed fruit.

Receiving: If available, check the Lot Number, Grower Number, Packing Date and weigh boxes. There can be wide variances of acceptable defects, red color, sizing and weights. Good growers pack a nice box of fruit, while others take advantage of the fact there are no standardized U.S. grades. Open boxes and inspect fruit for brown rot and mold around the base of the stem and the bottom. Brown russeting, open cracks or dry, wrinkled skin are all symptoms of age. Cut open, sample and check for brown rot. Reject shipments in general with an accumulation of more than 10% defects.

Raspberries

Grades: No.1/Domestic
Packs: 4.4oz|6oz|1 pint|2 pint|18oz|1 quart
Cartons: 1.36kg/3#|2kg/4.4#|4kg/8.8#|4.54kg/10#
Store: Refrigerated|Optimum Temperature +1C/33F

Remarks: Raspberries require gentle handling, rotate regularly and pull down at close to avoid excessive shrink, culling and repacking.

Displaying: Dummy displays. If Raspberries are attracting fruit flies, place a small portable fan behind the display (the fan will blow them away). Firm berries will last several hours on display with little impact, ripe berries need to be moved quickly (cut displays if fruit is soft and ripe). Displaying fruit in refrigerated counters is best, although condensation can build up inside the clamshell lid and slow sales. Quantity pricing and cross selling with other berry varieties will increase sales.

Receiving: Raspberries are force-air cooled to extend shelf-life, good quality fruit looks bright, fresh and appetizing. Open clamshells and sample, inspect the white pads for red stains, this is usually an indication of aging fruit. Berries should feel firm not soft. Cases can spoil overnight if mold is found inside the center of just a few berries, this is an indication the fruit was picked after a heavy rainfall (a no-no). Reject dull looking, wet, moldy, or shrivelled fruit and shipments in general with an accumulation of more than 10% defects.

Star Fruit/Carambola

Grades: Graded by color|Stage 1 thru 7
Sizes: 15|18|20|24|28|30|32+
Cartons: 3.5kg/7.7#|9kg/20#|10kg/22#|14kg/30.8#
Store: Refrigerated|Optimum Temperature +5C/41F
Optimum Stage: 4 (breaking)|5 (yellow with green edges)

Remarks: Difficult to handle, due to the long ocean voyage star fruit must endure and often being stored improperly on arrival at the warehouse. It is almost impossible to receive good quality, either arriving too green or overripe.

Displaying: Star fruit can be stacked 2-3 layers high, however their ribs damage easily and turn brown, display in their styrofoam or cellophane packaging. Dummy displays during slow times. Green fruit does not sell at all and will breakdown before it ripens. Cull soft, spotted and bruised fruit, discount or use for fruit salad and samples. Throw out as a last resort.

Receiving: If available, check the Lot Number, Grower Number and Packing Date on the boxes. Open and inspect ribs for brown edges, spotting, mold and chilling injury (soft ribs with translucent flesh). Solid green fruit and fruit with yellow edges should be rejected. Good quality star fruit can be stored for up to 2-3 weeks in a wet cooler (+90% RH). Most supermarkets do not have wet coolers, expect fruit to last 2-3 days in a normal cooler. In general, reject shipments with an accumulation of more than 10% defects, with star fruit there will have to be some leeway.

Strawberries

Grades: No.1 | Combo | No.2
Packs: Pint | 1# | 2# | 4# | 1/2 Flat | Full Flat
Cartons: 2.27kg/5# | 3.64kg/8# | 4.54kg/10#
Store: Refrigerated | Optimum Temperature +1C/33F

Remarks: Strawberries sales are a big part of the produce department. Rotate regularly and pull down at close to avoid excessive shrink, culling and repacking.

Displaying: Most supermarkets have moved to clamshells, reducing handling and shrink; fruit can be stacked several layers high with little impact (cut displays during slow times). Displaying in a refrigerated counter is best, although condensation can build up inside the clamshell lid and slow sales. Quantity pricing and cross selling with other berry varieties will increase sales.

Receiving: Strawberries can be a difficult and time consuming fruit to handle when poor quality is received. If available, check the Lot Number, Grower Number and Packing Date on flats. Open clamshells, sample, and inspect for overripe berries, mold, slime and wetness; all indications of age. Berries should be firm not soft, wrinkled fruit is usually a sign of chilling injury caused by the truck reefer or warehouse cooler (page 23, diagram 5D). Fruit can spoil overnight if mold is found on just a few berries. Reject dull looking, wet, moldy, or shrivelled fruit and shipments in general with an accumulation of more than 10% defects.

Watermelon

Grades: Fancy | No.1 | No.2 | Orchard Run
Sizes: 3 | 4 | 5 | 6 | 8+
Cases: Personal 34# | Seedless 40-50# | Seeded 60-70#
Bins: 182kg/400# | 364kg/800#
Store: Unrefrigerated | Optimum Temperature +10C/50F

Remarks: Easy to handle, watermelon should be pulled down at night and kept in a cool storage area. Once fruit becomes overripe it is difficult to move.

Displaying: Watermelon should be sold on the firm side. Shoppers wanting ripe melons that can be eaten immediately, can always be steered towards the sliced ½'s and ¼'s. Cull slightly overripe fruit, sell as slices, fruit salad or use for sampling. Throw out as necessary.

Receiving: If available, check the Lot Number, Grower Number, Packing Date and Count. There can be big weight discrepancies between watermelon labels. Stores retailing watermelon by the pound should always weigh the boxes and bins. Your store may be losing substantial money. Report grossly underweight labels to the Purchaser. Inspect for softness and bruising, usually signs of overripe fruit. Press your thumbs firmly against the rind, fruit should be solid; a slight softness is a sign the melons are ripe. A few ripe melons are okay, an entire shipment is not. Melons should look bright, clean and healthy; a dull appearance can be a sign of ripe and overripe fruit. Cut open, inspect flesh and sample melons. Reject shipments in general with an accumulation of more than 10% defects.

Chapter 8

Vegetables
(In alphabetical order)

Overview: Vegetables are usually broken down into sub-categories and displayed alongside each other accordingly. This is an time proven method that works well and allows you to learn and manage your section effectively.

We will use the onion category as an example...by displaying onions alongside each other, you will quickly ascertain which varieties are "key" items and which are "dogs" (slow movers). Yellow "medium" size onions are the biggest mover, sold either in 3lb bags or loose. However in-season yellow "jumbo sweets" are in high demand and can outsell the medium size.

The Produce Department is the least boring section of a supermarket. A can of soup is just that...a can of soup. Produce selection and varieties are constantly changing as one season begins and another ends. Shoppers happily look forward to these changes

- Sweet Peas in May
- New Dug Potatoes in July
- Local Green Tomatoes in August
- Canning Peaches and Pears in September
- Hard-shell Squash picked after the first frost
- Pumpkins for Halloween
- Brussel Sprouts on the Stalk for Thanksgiving

Common Quality Problems

Quality issues abound in produce and finding the right labels, growers, countries and varieties is a learning experience. Some... labels are known to pack the best lettuce... growers produce the best tomatoes... countries known to have the best climate... varieties have more flavor.

Building big displays to move problem inventory can sometimes end up creating more headaches than being a solution. It is wiser to have a dedicated Produce Clerk taking care of the problem product. Quantity pricing and cross-selling will help move the oversupply.

Tip Burn: A common problem during summer months with all varieties of lettuces. This is usually caused by a calcium deficiency, although warmer weather conditions can also be responsible. There is not much you can do when this problem runs rampant in certain growing regions, except cut displays until quality improves. Put up a blurb on your signage explaining to shoppers that quality has been affected by Mother Nature and is not a purchasing problem. The number one produce complaint in supermarkets is lettuce related.

Black/Core Rot: A symptom of age, lettuces and celery should be rejected upon arrival if this problem is evident. Sometimes trimming the butts will solve the problem, but the shelf-life is practically non-existent; you need to move product quickly. Product should be displayed on a cold counter, otherwise dummy displays.

Hollow Cores/Brown Heart: Product can look beautiful on arrival, inspect the butts and suddenly you realize there is a problem. A symptom common to broccoli and cauliflower caused by over-fertilizing or a boron deficiency. Product should be rejected on arrival, but if it is missed and you are stuck with inventory… trim and cut up into florets to move.

Chinese Veggies: Over-mature product will have open-flowers, a milky substance visible on the bottom of the stalks and butts (or both). Unscrupulous growers count on the fact that most supermarket chains are not well-trained in the quality issues associated with Chinese veggies. Product showing these symptoms should be rejected.

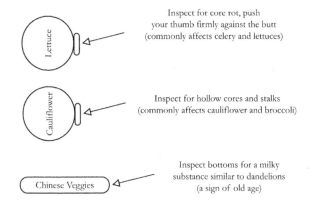

Diagram 9A:

Black or Hollow cores are a sign of age

Lettuce — Inspect for core rot, push your thumb firmly against the butt (commonly affects celery and lettuces)

Cauliflower — Inspect for hollow cores and stalks (commonly affects cauliflower and broccoli)

Chinese Veggies — Inspect bottoms for a milky substance similar to dandelions (a sign of old age)

Artichokes (Globe)

Grades: No.1 Reg/Long|No.2|Extra Class|Class 1|Class 2
Sizes: Baby|Medium|Large|Jumbo
Counts: 15|18|24|30|36|48|60|112
Cartons: 5.45kg/12# | 9kg/20# Standard
Store: Refrigerated|Optimum Temperature +1C/33F

Remarks: Relatively easy to handle, artichokes have thorns on the tips of their leaves; be careful not to prick yourself. Sold by each, know your customers and offer the right sizes. Small sizes (36/48) are more economical and purchased by Italian and Middle-Eastern peoples.

Displaying: Artichokes will begin to breakdown after a couple of hours on display (the leaves will start to blacken). Best to display on a bed of crushed ice, standing up (wet counter sprayers tend to drench the artichokes). It may be necessary to trim the butts several times daily because they oxidize (rust) rapidly and look unattractive. Trim lightly. Cull brown and dried out product, bag up and discount. Blackening artichokes should be thrown out.

Receiving: Check Count and weigh boxes if they look light. Open and inspect for brown/black discoloration, softness and shrivelling. Artichokes should be firm, heavy and have a healthy green appearance (a purplish tinge is okay). Ugly stem bottoms is normal as long as there is no discoloration in the stems. Also, inspect for mold on top of the artichoke and the bottom where the stem attaches itself to the bulb. Reject shipments in general with an accumulation of more than 10% defects.

Asparagus

Grades: No.1 | No.2
Sizes: Pencil | Small | Standard | Large | Jumbo | Colossal
Cartons: 5kg/11# | 6.82kg/15# | 9kg/20# | 12.73kg/28#
Store: Refrigerated | Optimum Temperature +3-4C/38-40F

Remarks: Easy to handle, Asparagus is a big seller. To determine how much of a stalk is tender and edible, snap stalks at their bottoms. Smaller sizes (pencil, small and standard) are more desirable.

Displaying: Displaying bunched asparagus standing up in tubs of water (one inch of water) is the best method. Product can last all day in clean water. Displaying on ice or wet counters works too but is not as effective; the tips will still dry out faster. Asparagus can be left in their tubs when put back into the cooler at close.

White Asparagus: Highly perishable, avoid unnecessary handling. Touching stalks will cause them to snap. Display packaged if possible to avoid loses. Cover at close to avoid stalks turning green (like potatoes).

Receiving: If available, check the Lot Number, Grower Number and Packing Date. Open and smell tips, rotten tips will stink. Asparagus with seedy tips needs to be sold in 1-2 days. Check for mold, shrivelled stalks and color; white-purplish stalks are tough and undesirable. Product with these common defects can still be sold (except rotten tips). Use your judgement or ask your supervisor if you are unsure. Reject shipments in general with an accumulation of more than 10% defects.

Beans Green/Yellow

Grades: Fancy | No.1 | No.2
Cartons: 4.54kg/10# | 6.82kg/15# | 11.36kg/25# | 28-30#
Bags: 8oz | 12oz | 1# | 2#
Store: Refrigerated | Optimum Temperature +1C/33F

Remarks: Fresh beans need to be rotated regularly to minimize shrink. Round varieties are usually more tender, hold up and sell better than flat varieties. Sales can be substantial during summer months when local supply is being harvested and readily available.

Displaying: Turn off sprayers if product is being displayed in a wet counter. Beans turn rusty quickly if they are regularly being sprayed with water (especially yellow). Displays should be dummied at all times to ensure freshness, shoppers are very finicky when purchasing beans. This also makes proper rotation much easier. Retailing random weight bags is also a great method to move volume and reduce shrink. Cull soft, wrinkled, and rusty beans, bag up and discount.

Receiving: If available, check the Lot Number, Grower Number and Packing Date. Open and inspect beans for rust, clumps of mold, shrivelling and wetness. Press your thumb against the tips, if they snap off cleanly, this is a sign of freshness. Wet beans will turn rusty quickly. Remove plastic pallet wrap to avoid sweating. Do not store beans in front of cooler fans or they may get chilled (page 23, diagram 5D). Reject wet beans and shipments in general with an accumulation of more than 10% defects.

Beets

Grades: No.1 | No.2
Cartons: 12's | 24's | 11.36kg/25# | 22.73kg/50#
Retail Bags: 1.36kg/3# | 2.27kg/5# | 4.54kg/10#
Store: Refrigerated | Optimum Temperature +1C/33F

Remarks: Easy to handle, Beet sales are limited. Round beets are more popular than the elongated tubular type, except during pickling season (they fit into the jars easier). During pickling season (August/September) when local supply is readily available, offering 5lb/10lb bags will increase sales (either tubular or baby/small sized round beets).

Displaying: Beets dry out quickly if not hydrated regularly, display on a wet counter. Keep displays small. The tops and bottoms may occasionally require trimming. Bunched beets are popular with shoppers that love to eat the leaves like spinach. Yellow, gold and candy-striped beet varieties are much sweeter and have become popular (both bulk and bunched). Cull soft, wrinkled and moldy beets, bag up and discount.

Receiving: Bulk beets should be clean, solid and super firm on arrival. Dirty plastic bags can be an indication of possible quality issues. Inspect around the stem and bottom for slime or mold. Ugly or wrinkled product will not sell well. Bunched beets should have clean, vibrant green leaves. Decayed or yellowing leaves are signs of age. Reject shipments in general with an accumulation of more than 10% defects.

Bok Choy

Grades: No U.S. or International
Cartons: 4.54kg/10# | 9kg/20# | 25# | 30# | 40# | 50# | 60#
Store: Refrigerated | Optimum Temperature +1C/33F

Remarks: Bok Choy can be difficult to handle, sales are limited (even in heavily populated Asian areas). Asians prefer baby varieties of bok choy and prices have dropped significantly as production increases in the U.S. and Mexico.

Displaying: Price sensitive, overcharging will stifle sales. Bok choy wilts easily and should be displayed on a wet counter. The colder the better, bok choy does not get chilled. Product should be banded or taped. Bagging is time consuming, costly and the product will sweat and breakdown faster. Cull product that is wilted, spotted or has yellowing leaves. Bag up and sell cheap.

Baby Bok & Shanghai Choy: Similar procedures should be used when retailing and handling these varieties. However product is better marketed in random weight cellophane bags. Turn off sprayers and avoid fans blowing directly on the product or the bags will condensate and need to be rebagged.

Receiving: Weigh boxes. Open and inspect for tip burn, yellow leaves, black spots along the stalks, and wet, brown cores (page 105, diagram 9A). Bok choy should be bright, crisp with clean butts. Reject wilted product and shipments in general with an accumulation of more than 10% defects.

Broccoli

Grades: Fancy | No.1 | No.2
Counts: 14 | 18
Bunched: 11.36kg/25# **Crowns:** 9kg/20#
Florets Bags: 12oz | 2# | 1.36kg/3# | 2.27kg/5#
Store: Refrigerated | Optimum Temperature +1C/33F

Remarks: Easy to handle, Broccoli is a staple of the Produce Department. Distressed product can usually be trimmed, cut into Florets and sold at regular price (clean and soak the florets in the back sink before putting up).

Displaying: Bunched Broccoli should be displayed on a bed of ice; otherwise the wet counter will work nicely. Rotate regularly to avoid extra culling and waste. Once product starts to breakdown, the odor can be distracting and needs to be taken care of quickly. Quantity pricing will help move inventory. Cull wilted, decayed and flowering product, throw out, bag up and discount, or cut into florets (use your judgement and work accordingly).

Receiving: Boxes should arrive properly iced. Open and smell for the rancorous stink of decay. Inspect broccoli for hollow stalks and brown heart (page 105, diagram 9A). Hollow crowns should also be rejected. Check heads for signs of mold, decay and flowering (yellowing). Wilted stalks are a sign of age. Bunched broccoli, crowns and florets should be iced before being put away in the cooler. Reject shipments in general with an accumulation of more than 10% defects.

Brussel Sprouts

Grades: No.1 | No.2
Cartons: 11.36kg/25# Standard
Bags: 8oz | 12oz | 1# | 2#
Store: Refrigerated | Optimum Temperature +1C/33F

Remarks: Easy to handle. Brussel Sprouts are critical for the Thanksgiving Holiday, not so much for Christmas or Easter. Sales are limited during the rest of the year.

Displaying: Brussel sprouts should be displayed on a bed of ice; otherwise the wet counter will work nicely. Rotate 1-2 times daily depending on movement. Keep displays minimal. Once product starts to breakdown, the odor can be distracting and needs to be taken care of quickly. Cull brussel sprouts with yellowing leaves and ugly brown butts, bag up and discount. Throw out decayed product.

Brussel Sprouts on the Stalk: These taste fresher and make the perfect addition to the Produce Department during the Holidays. Shoppers are always happy to see new items that will help make their Holiday dinners more enjoyable. Retail by the each (quantity price too).

Receiving: Boxes should arrive iced. Open and smell for the stink of decay. Inspect product for signs of mold, decay and yellowing leaves. Brussel sprouts should be iced before being put away in the cooler. Reject shipments with ugly butts and shipments in general with an accumulation of more than 10% defects.

Cabbage

Grades: No.1 | No.2
Cartons: 11.36kg/25# | 15.91kg/35# | 18.18kg/40# | 50#
Bins: 227kg/500# | 454kg/1000#
Store: Refrigerated | Optimum Temperature +1C/33F

Remarks: Easy to handle. The heavier "winter" cabbage is most popular. Usually picked after the first frost to soften the hard veins in the heads. These varieties are used for cabbage rolls and sauerkraut. Chinese "flat" green cabbage has also become popular for making cabbage rolls because of their thinner leaves and great taste. 25lb/50lb sacks of these varieties should be offered during the month of September. European shoppers will purchase 1-20 bags.

Displaying: The lighter summer varieties of cabbage do not hold up well on the table (neither does savoy). Keep displays small. You will need to routinely trim the butts and remove the occasional leaves to keep product looking fresh. The heavier winter cabbage will roll off displays and their heads will crack if stacked too high (deterring sales). Cull ugly heads and sell as ½'s, for sauerkraut or slaw. Throw out as a last resort.

Receiving: Smell for decay, open and inspect for cracked and split heads. Look for signs of insects and worms (holes in the leaves), mold, decay and yellowing leaves. Product with ugly butts is a sign of age, but can be trimmed if the rest of the head looks fine. Reject old, pale, shrivelled, ugly looking cabbage and shipments in general with an accumulation of more than 10% defects.

Carrots

Grades: No.1 | No.2
Sizes: Baby | Medium | Jumbo
Bags: 2# | 1.36kg/3# | 2.27kg/5# | 4.54kg/10# | 25# | 50#
Cartons: 10kg/22# | 11.36kg/25# | 18kg/40#
Peeled: 1# | 2# | 5#
Store: Refrigerated | Optimum Temperature +1C/33F

Remarks: Easy to handle. Carrots are a staple of the Produce Department. During summer months shoppers look to purchase baby and small sized sweet Nante type carrots for pickling, canning and fresh eating. Usually available in 10lb retail bags while supplies last.

Displaying: Loose (bulk) and bunched carrots should be displayed on a wet counter, otherwise they will become dry, wrinkle and need to be thrown out. Rotate regularly (especially bunched) to avoid extra culling and waste. Baby peeled and formed carrots need to be kept refrigerated as per Health Regulations. Turn off sprayers to keep bags from becoming soaked and condensation setting in. Cello bags of carrots can be displayed on tables, but product will eventually dry out if it is not rotated a couple of times daily. Quantity pricing always helps move inventory.

Receiving: Boxes can be top iced. Inspect for mold, shoots sprouting from the tops, black tips and shrivelling. Carrots should be bright and clean, cut open and check cores for black discoloration. Broken carrots sell well for juicing. Reject shipments in general with an accumulation of more than 10% defects.

Cauliflower

Grades: No.1 | No.2/Commercial
Counts: 9 | 12 | 16
Cartons: 11.36kg-13.64kg/25-30#
Florets Bags: 12oz | 2# | 1.36kg/3# | 2.27kg/5#
Store: Refrigerated | Optimum Temperature +1C/33F

Remarks: Easy to handle, Cauliflower large (12's) and jumbo (9's) sizes sell best; sales slow when offering medium size (16's). Distressed product can usually be trimmed, cut into Florets and sold at regular price (clean and soak the florets in the back sink before putting up).

Displaying: Cauliflower can be displayed on tables or wet counters (turn off sprayers to prevent condensation). Rotate regularly, once product starts to breakdown the odor can be overpowering. Quantity pricing will help move inventory. Cull heads that show signs of mold, spots, decay (minor spotting is okay) or yellowing leaves. Throw out, bag up and discount, or cut into florets as required.

Colored Cauliflower: Purple and Orange cauliflower have become popular; the Green (broccoflower) is so-so. Use the same procedures handling colored varieties, when cutting up florets try mixing all the colors together.

Receiving: Inspect for hollow stem and brown heart (page 105, diagram 9A). Check for mold, black spots, decay and yellow leaves. Curds should be tight, compact and the heads should feel heavy. Reject shipments in general with an accumulation of more than 10% defects.

Celery

Grades: Extra No.1 | No.1 | No.1 Heart | No.2
Counts: 18 | 24 | 30 | 36 | 48 **Hearts:** 12 | 18
Cartons: 22.73-25kg/50-55# **Hearts:** 13.64kg/30#
Store: Refrigerated | Optimum Temperature +1C/33F

Remarks: Easy to handle, Celery 24's are the industry standard, sales slow when selling smaller sizes by each. Distressed product can usually be trimmed, cut into celery sticks and sold at regular price.

Displaying: Celery should be displayed banded or sleeved. Product displayed at room temperature will eventually dry out if not rotated regularly. Better to display on an iced table or wet counter. Quantity pricing is an excellent method to move inventory. Celery can be stacked several layers high with little impact. Cull product that shows signs of decay, spotting or yellowing leaves. Bag up and discount, cut into celery sticks, or throw out as required.

Celery Hearts: Packaged Celery Hearts have steady sales and a small display on the wet counter should always be maintained (turn off sprayer). Quantity pricing does not significantly increase sales.

Receiving: Inspect for core rot, hollow stems (page 105, diagram 9A), mold, spotting, decay and yellow leaves. Light green is better. Beautiful celery with yellow leaves will breakdown quickly. Open bunch and inspect center for black heart. Reject shipments in general with an accumulation of more than 10% defects.

Corn

Grades: Fancy | Fancy Husked | No.1 | No.1 Husked | No.2
Sizes: 48's/28-30#s | 60's/38-40#
Store: Refrigerated | Optimum Temperature +1C/33F

Remarks: Easy to handle, corn is a huge part of summer sales. Due to high shrink and ad promotions most grocery chains end up showing an annual loss. The Bi-color (Peaches n' Cream) varieties sell best.

Displaying: Corn is best displayed on an iced table, product can become drenched on wet counters. Keep a water spray bottle nearby to spray the display occasionally. Rotate to reduce losses. When restocking, try putting display stock in bags of 6's and 12's. Shoppers in a hurry will usually take a bag instead of wasting time sorting through the display. Displays can be heaped during busy times and when quantity pricing is implemented. Cull product that shows signs of decay, mold, black tips, pink or green mold, or mechanical damage from harvesting. Bag up and discount, or throw out as required.

Packaged Corn: This is an excellent addition during winter months. Quantity pricing will increase sales.

Receiving: Inspect for worms, there will be a sawdust appearance on the tips. Check butts for dryness and mold, a reddish-pink color means the corn is very old. Cobs should feel heavy and be free of mechanical damage and brown discoloration. Reject shipments in general with an accumulation of more than 10% defects.

Cucumbers

Grades: Fancy | Extra No.1 | No.1 Small | No.1 Medium
No.1 Large | No.1 Extra Large | No.2
Dills: 20# | 25# | 40# **English** 12s | 18s **Field:** 24s | 48s | 60s
Store: Unrefrigerated | Optimum Temperature +10C/50F
Store: Dill & Bread n' Butter | Refrigerate +1C/33F

Remarks: Easy to handle, display cukes beside tomatoes to increase sales. Persian cukes have become very popular. Cull product with overly soft, mushy or yellowing tips. Cukes begin to smell, develop mold and become slimy as they age. Bag up and discount, or throw out as required.

Field Cukes (Slicers) are usually waxed and will begin to feel very waxy (slowing sales) if left on display too long. Dummy displays to minimize shrink. Burpless varieties are available to shoppers that suffer from indigestion.

Long English Cukes can be heaped with little impact. Quantity pricing will help move significant volume.

Dill/Bread n' Butter are very perishable and breakdown rapidly in plastic bags. Display on wet counter to minimize losses. During pickling season (August/September) dill cukes are in big demand, shoppers can purchase 5-100lbs at a time.

Receiving: Smell for decay. Easily chilled, cukes should be firm, especially at the tips. Reject cukes with black mold, an unhealthy yellow pallor and in general with an accumulation of more than 10% defects.

Eggplant

Grades: Fancy | No.1 | No.2
Counts: 18ct & 24ct Standard | Volume Fill Asian
Cartons: 11.36kg/25# Standard | 13.64kg/30# Asian
Store: Refrigerated | Optimum Temperature +10C/50F

Remarks: Price sensitive and sometimes difficult to handle, Eggplant have thorny tops, handle delicately to avoid injury. The first signs of decay often appear on their tops (under leaves). The Italian variety is the most common type grown and sold. However, many growers today have switched to seedless varieties similar in appearance that are more desirable. Display on table or wet counter. Eggplant chill easily, ensure cold air is not blowing directly on product. Cull floppy, wrinkled, moldy and marked up product, bag up and discount.

Italian Eggplant should be displayed with their wrapper around the bottoms. This prevents product from rubbing against each other; causing bruising and ugly brown marks.

Asian: Easier to handle, Asian varieties are elongated. Some light scabbing is okay, but wrinkled tips are signs of old age and product should be culled from displays.

Receiving: Inspect for softness, mold (check under top leaves), wrinkling, and scabs. Eggplant should feel firm. Chilling…brown discoloration sometimes hard to identify on the dark purple skin. Remove plastic pallet wrap to prevent sweating. Reject shipments in general with an accumulation of more than 10% defects.

119

Gai Lon/Yu Choy

Grades: No.1 | No.2 (Unofficial)
Cartons: 4.54kg/10# | 9kg/20# | 25# | 30# | 35# | 40#
Store: Refrigerated | Optimum Temperature +1C/33F

Remarks: Chinese vegetables have an unofficial grading system. No.1 grade usually has medium to small stalks, flower buds are tightly closed with some uniformity. The product should look bright, clean and have a nice sheen. No.2 grade, the product can be more mature, which means the stalks will be tough. Tough stalks have more to do with the age of the plants than the size of the stalks. Very similar to asparagus, snap the bottoms to determine how much of the stalk is tender and edible. If the tough ends are peeled, the whole stalk can be eaten.

Displaying: Asians will pay more for excellent quality, but overcharging will stifle sales. Product should be taped or banded, their bottoms trimmed and even (like asparagus). Retailing in cellophane bags is better. Best displayed on a wet counter (turn off sprayers). Cull product that is wilted, spotted, yellowing or flowering. Bag up and sell cheap.

Receiving: Weigh boxes. Check for yellow leaves and spotting along the stalks. Reject product with milky bottoms (page 105, diagram 9A). Product should be bright, crisp with clean butts and tightly closed flower buds. Gai Lon has white flowers and Yu Choy has yellow flowers. Blooming is a sign of over maturity and it will not sell. Reject wilted product and shipments in general with an accumulation of more than 10% defects.

Garlic

Grades: No.1 | Unclassified | Commercial
Sizes: Giant | Jbo | X-Jbo | Super Jbo | Colossal | Super Colossal
China Sizes: 4.5cm | 5.0cm | 5.5cm | 6.0cm | 6.5cm
Cartons: 5kg/11# | 10kg/22# | 13.64kg/30# | 20kg/44#
Bags: 2ct | 3ct | 4ct | 5ct | 500g | 1kg
Store: Refrigerated | Optimum Temperature +1C/33F

Remarks: I prefer to refrigerate garlic. Most supermarkets today offer Chinese garlic because of its low cost and high return. Garlic sells better by the pound. Purple varieties have more flavor. Many upscale markets and stores offer Russian and German purple varieties to their discerning customers. Grown locally by small farm operations (much more expensive).

Displaying: Easy to handle, dummy displays to avoid messy clean-ups (page 14, diagram 3C). When in a hurry, it is simple enough to rotate dummied boxes forward as you restock. Messy displays slow sales. Cull garlic that is soft, dry, moldy or sprouting, bag up and discount.

Garlic Scapes/Stems: Similar to chives, good shelf-life and delicious. Display on the wet counter. Should be sold banded or taped in bunches.

Receiving: Weigh boxes, check Lot and Grower Number and Packing Date. Garlic should be hard and look fresh. Bulbs with excessive dry skins, dried out cloves, sprouting, mold or shrivelling should be rejected and shipments in general with an accumulation of more than 10% defects.

Ginger Root

Grades: No.1 | No.2 | Commercial
Sizes: 50g | 100-150g | 150-200g | 200-250g | 250-300g | 300g+
Cartons: 10kg/22# | 13.64kg/30# | 20kg/44#
Store: Unrefrigerated | Optimum Temperature +10C/50F

Remarks: Ginger Root like bananas is actually sold by the "Hand" size. Bigger Hands are more expensive. Most supermarkets today retail Chinese ginger because of its low cost. The best ginger is grown in Hawaii.

Displaying: Easy to handle, ginger can be left out on displays for days with little impact. Dummy displays to avoid messy clean-ups. When in a hurry, it is simple enough to rotate dummied boxes forward as you restock. Messy displays slow sales. Cull broken, soft, wet, moldy and wrinkled pieces, bag up and sell cheap.

Young Gingers/Sushi Gingers: These four varieties are very perishable, display on the wet counter. Young ginger has green shoots that deteriorate quickly. Products are pricier and retailing in small cellophane bags (turn off sprayers) is a good idea.

Receiving: Do not drop boxes or the ginger will break. Ginger is usually underweight, weigh boxes (2lbs under is normal and acceptable). Open and inspect for wetness, mold, shrivelling and broken pieces. Wet soaked (soggy) ginger is a common problem and not acceptable. Pieces should be shiny, dry and unbroken (broken pieces will not sell). Reject shipments in general with an accumulation of more than 10% defects.

Green Onions

Grades: No.1 | No.2
Cartons: 48ct Standard
Store: Refrigerated | Optimum Temperature +1C/33F

Remarks: Green Onions should be displayed on a wet counter; a bed of ice increases shelf-life. Keep a pair of small scissors handy, sometimes it is necessary to trim the tops for appearance sake.

Displaying: Easy to handle, green onions need to be rotated regularly to minimize shrink. When stocking displays, remove ugly, decayed, ripped or damaged stalks from bunch. Quantity pricing will significantly increase sales. Culled green onions stock cannot usually be reduced and sold; throw out as necessary.

Received without Ice: Green onions should arrive packed in a good 10-15lbs of ice, be suspicious of arrivals without ice. Inspect stalks closely for discoloration, at a casual glance they look fine but can surprisingly turn bad overnight. Turn boxes over, open bottoms and inspect the bottom layers, here is where the problems will be most apparent. A strong odor is a dead giveaway that the stock is old. Curled stalks and black tips are also signs of old age.

Receiving: Iced product may need to be topped off with more ice before being put away. Store next to floor drain in cooler to allow for water run-off (slippery cooler floors can be dangerous). Reject shipments in general with an accumulation of more than 10% defects.

Herbs Fresh

Grades: No U.S. or International
Counts: 12|24|48|60
Packs: Bunched|Bagged|Clamshell|Potted
Store: Refrigerated|Optimum Temperature +1C/33F

Remarks: Fresh herbs have become a necessity in the Produce Department as shoppers demand better selection and availability. Usually we throw out more than we sell, most supermarkets run a minimum 50% shrink. Packaged herbs are the easiest to handle and retail, although potted herbs need little attention except the occasional watering and do not require refrigeration.

Packaged: Easy to handle, herbs need to be rotated regularly to minimize culls. Best-selling varieties are basil, dill and rosemary (the others are all dogs). Packaged savory should be offered for Thanksgiving (stuffing). Quantity pricing should be implemented. Culled herbs cannot usually be reduced, throw out as required.

Bunched: Parsley, Cilantro, Watercress (remove slugs) and Italian Parsley hold up better in tubs of water (one inch high) just like asparagus. Otherwise product should be displayed on a wet counter (rotate regularly to avoid drenching from sprayers).

Receiving: Herbs chill easily, packaged herbs should look clean, fresh and be free of condensation. Bunched herbs should arrive top iced just like green onions. Reject shipments of yellow, pale, wilted, decayed, or chilled herbs.

Horseradish Fresh

Grades: No.1 (Thick Roots) | No.2 (Thin Roots)
Cartons: 1# packaged | 4.54kg/10# Box | 50# Sack
Store: Refrigerated | Optimum Temperature +1C/33F

Remarks: Fresh Horseradish Root should be carried during pickling season (August/September). Europeans require this product to add heat to their sauerkraut and other pickled vegetables. There is usually a huge price savings per pound, when you purchase 50lb sacks instead of 10lb boxes (the savings can be up to 50%).

Displaying: Horseradish is usually purchased pre-washed and cleaned; but this is not always the case. Sometimes you will be required to soak and wash the dirt off, before displaying this product on the wet counter. Product needs to be re-hydrated so the sprayers are ideal. The bottoms usually need to be lightly trimmed before putting up. Do not cut roots into smaller pieces for customers. They do not want to pay for the slender tops of the root and are hoping they can fool you by saying the piece is too big.

Receiving: Horseradish is expensive, weigh the boxes. Sometimes product has been stored at the warehouse for a long time, expect the boxes to be slightly underweight (10% is okay). Horseradish should feel solid and heavy. A small amount of soil is okay, too much and you are paying for dirt instead of product. A little bit of white mold on the bottoms is normal too and can easily be trimmed away. Horseradish that is speckled with mold, sprouting new roots or is shrivelled should be rejected.

Lettuce Head

Grades: Fancy | No.1 | No.2
Counts: 24 | 30
Cartons: 15.91kg/35# Cello | 22.73kg/50# Naked
Store: Refrigerated | Optimum Temperature +1C/33F

Remarks: Easy to handle. Head (Iceberg) lettuce is more commonly referred to as Cello Lettuce. Sales have slowed as shoppers switch to more convenient packaged salads.

Displaying: Most supermarkets list Cello lettuce to keep labor costs low. Naked lettuce needs to be trimmed and wrapped and should be soaked in cold water (10-20 min) before being put up. Lettuce can be stacked (butts down) several layers high with little impact. Displaying beside tomatoes, cukes and quantity pricing will increase sales. Rotate regularly. Tip Burn (page 104) can be a headache during summer months. 24's sell best, switching to 30's will slow sales. However when lettuces are expensive, the price spread often makes it worthwhile. Cull distressed heads and discount.

Receiving: Inspect for signs of russeting, slime and shrivelling. Russeting on leaves (especially around the butt) usually means the problems persist throughout the interior of the head and should be rejected. Check for core rot (page 105, diagram 9A) by firmly pressing your thumb against the butt. Although many stores like the feel of a heavy head of lettuce, lighter heads are actually better quality. Reject rusty lettuce and shipments in general with an accumulation of more than 10% defects.

Lettuce Leaf

Grades: Fancy | No.1 | No.2
Counts: 12 | 18 | 24 | 30
Cartons: 18kg/40# Romaine
Store: Refrigerated | Optimum Temperature +1C/33F

Remarks: Romaine and Green Leaf make up the majority of Leaf Lettuce sales. Overall, movement has slowed as shoppers switch to more convenient packaged salads. Hot House Butter lettuce has a regular following, field grown does not sell as well. Red Leaf, Endive and Escarole varieties are more trouble than they are worth, shrink is easily 50-80%. Quantity pricing will help reduce losses on these varieties. .

Displaying: Display on wet counters and tables, lettuces should be banded or wrapped. Do not over-trim butts, you may need to re-trim them again later on. If the product is not sold within a couple of hours, the butt ends will oxidize (turn rusty again) and require re-trimming. Rotate regularly to reduce handling. Displaying in close proximity to tomatoes and cukes will increase sales. Tip Burn (page 104) can be a headache during summer months. Cull distressed product and sell cheap.

Receiving: Inspect leaves for mold, slime, insect damage, shrivelling, tip burn and rusty discoloration. Check for core rot (page 105, diagram 9A) by firmly pressing your thumb against the butt. Spread apart leaves and inspect centers for black hearts. Reject shipments in general with an accumulation of more than 10% defects.

Lettuce Salad Mixes

Grades: Food Safety Guidelines must be adhered to
Bags: 6oz | 8oz | 12oz | 1# | 2# | 1.36kg/3# | 2.72kg/5#
Store: Refrigerated | Optimum Temperature +1C/33F

Remarks: A wide array of pack sizes and salad mixes is available today. Deciding which ones are best suited for your supermarket is a costly lesson. Products usually deteriorate before their "Best Before" date. The clear winners here are the Consumers and Producers. Shrink can easily be 50%. This category continues to grow annually, the costs of production have dropped significantly, but new food safety measures and traceability (to avoid the next E. coli outbreak) initiatives are eating up these savings.

Displaying: Easy to handle, display on cold counters. Fans blowing directly on the packages may cause condensation inside the bags, slowing sales. Rotate regularly to minimize losses. Giving equal shelf space will increase shrink, shelf space should be prioritized based on movement. Quantity pricing and displaying in close proximity to tomatoes and cukes will increase sales. Cull distressed product and discount.

Receiving: Condensation is generally a sign the product has been sitting out somewhere or the truck driver had the reefer turned off. Check the "Best Before" date to make sure you have ample time to sell. Look for shrivelling, slime, mold and dryness. Always give Spring mix and Spinach extra attention and inspect closely. Repacking is difficult, reject problem shipments.

Mushrooms
White/Brown

Grades: No.1 | No.2 (Pizza)
Sizes: 200g | 8oz | 250g | 454g/16oz | 2.72kg/5# | 10#
Store: Refrigerated | Optimum Temperature +2-4C/35-39F

Remarks: Easy to handle, mushroom quality usually becomes a problem when it arrives in so-so condition. Inventory backs up affecting good arrivals too.

Displaying: Good quality sells quickly without concern. Mushrooms should be displayed on a cold or wet counter (turn off sprayers), ensure cold air is not blowing directly on bulk product. Stacking cello packages will cause bruising, display packages standing up if you are short of shelf space. Product can turn quickly on display (especially bulk), rotate every couple of hours. When replenishing bulk displays, try paper-bagging old stock for quick sales; shoppers in a hurry can just take-an-go. Discount as a last resort.

Receiving: Mushrooms are usually grown locally, boxes should not be underweight. Inspect for chilling (reefer fans blowing directly on product), mushroom veils should be tight, closed and stems firm. A small amount of discoloration is okay, but overall…blemish free. Product should look fresh and feel heavy in the palm of your hand. Remove plastic pallet wrap to prevent sweating, but leave on their protective sheet of paper covering the mushrooms. Reject product that you are uncomfortable accepting. If unsure, ask your supervisor.

Mushrooms Specialty

Grades: No.1 | No.2
Sizes: 100g | 125g | 150g | 200g | 8oz | 250g | 16oz | 500g | 3# | 5#
Favorites: Portabella | Oyster | Enoki | Shiitake | Crimini
Store: Refrigerated | Optimum Temperature +2-4C/35-39F

Remarks: Easy to handle, the Portabella and Crimini are popular enough to retail bulk too. The Shiitake, Oyster and Enoki are delicate varieties, break down and mold easily.

Displaying: Most supermarkets carry packages to reduce handling. Still…shrink can be substantial, do not overstock. Quantity pricing and cross-selling will help move excess inventory. Display on a cold or wet counter (turn off sprayers), ensure cold air is not blowing directly on bulk product. Stacking cello packages will cause bruising, display packages standing up if you are short of shelf space. Product can turn quickly on display (especially bulk), rotate every couple of hours. Cull distressed packages, bag up bulk and discount.

Receiving: Mushrooms are usually grown locally, boxes should not be underweight. Specialty mushrooms are susceptible to chilling, inspect closely. Mushroom veils should be tight, compact and closed, Look for a clean, fresh appearance with healthy stems. Remove plastic pallet wrap to prevent sweating, but leave on the protective sheet of paper covering the bulk. Reject product that you are uncomfortable accepting. If unsure, ask your supervisor.

Onions Overview

There are two distinct types of red, white and yellow onions... sweet varieties and the normal hot varieties. Easily identifiable, sweet varieties have flat tops and bottoms. Sweet onions are more expensive and unscrupulous growers will add or mislabel hot varieties as "sweets" to capitalize on the higher prices. This is a big customer complaint and supermarkets either look like they are misleading shoppers or incompetent.

Diagram 10A:

Sweet Onion Varieties

Tops and Bottoms
are flat not round

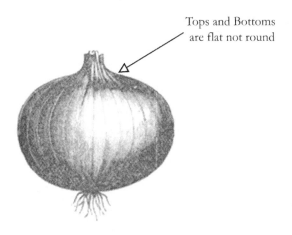

Popular Sweet Brands

- Walla Walla - Yellow (Washington)
- Texas 1015's – Yellow (Texas)
- Vidalia Sweets – Yellow (Georgia)
- Okanagan Sweets – Yellow (B.C., Canada)
- Maui Sweets – Yellow (Hawaii)
- Sweet Imperials – Yellow (California)
- Italian Sweets – Red (California)

Sweet varieties break down quickly. Once mold sets in to just a few onions, the entire shipment can turn overnight. Walla Walla is the worst for bad arrivals, followed by Texas 1015's. Many Packers should be more vigilant, they give the entire region a bad reputation. Inspect arrivals closely. Culling moldy displays is very time consuming, attracts fruit flies and you will have to deal with customer complaints and returns.

Displaying

Fruit flies are an indicator that you have quality issues on your display (find the source and remove). Place a small portable fan behind display to temporarily solve the problem (the fan blows them away). Loose onion skins build up over time and make displays look messy. Dummying displays will help manage this problem.

Onions can be heaped with little impact and adding the blurb "Sweet" to your signage will increase movement. Expensive varieties should be PLU'd, otherwise explain the differences to cashiers and leave a sample at the checkouts.

Receiving

Many Packers take advantage of high market prices for new crop onions and ship product before it is properly cured. This means the onions will break down on display much faster. New crop and sweet onions should always be refrigerated to reduce culling and waste.

"Winter" onions have been cured and can be stored at room temperature. By April...you should be getting out of winter storage supply. Quality problems will become more evident.

Shallots & Silverskins

Shallots are available year-round, though sales are insubstantial. Shoppers prefer large sizes (easier to peel). Silverskins are most in demand in the fall for pickling season. Baby Silverskins are preferred for pickling, the rest of the season carry large sizes (used mainly in stews).

Retailing in plastic bags will cause sweating, they will breakdown and mold rapidly. Netted bags and clamshells are much better.

Silverskins become moldy with black spotting and sprout green shoots as they age and become unsaleable. Shallots often look better at casual glance, the bulbs should always be firm. Squeeze between your fingers to determine their firmness, like Silverskins, mold and green shoots are signs of age and should be thrown out.

Onions Red

Grades: No.1 | No.2
Sizes: Boilers | Small | Medium | Jumbo | Colossal
Packs: 2# | 1.36kg/3# | 2.72kg/5# | 10# | 25# | 40# | 50#
Store: Refrigerated | Optimum Temperature +1C/33F
Onions Overview: Page 131

Remarks: Easy to handle, red onions can break down quickly; store in the cooler if space is available. Retailing bags does not significantly increase sales, often product sits and gets old. You may have to occasionally open bags and sell loose to keep stock fresh.

Displaying: Dummy displays for easy culling and restocking. Onions can be heaped with little impact. Displaying red, white and yellow onions together and cross-selling will increase sales. When the tips look dried out and brown; it may be necessary to cut the tips with a pair of scissors to maintain steady sales. Time consuming, only do this if you have extra time available. Cull distressed product, bag up and discount.

Receiving: Product should arrive dry, if the bags or boxes are wet...smell for a strong onion aroma (a sign of decay). If storing at room temperature, remove pallet wrap to prevent sweating and mold. Press your thumb firmly against the surface, onions should be very firm. Soft onions are old or may have been chilled. Inspect for mold (especially at the stem and root) and sprouting. Reject moldy or sprouting onions and shipments in general with an accumulation of more than 10% defects.

Onions White

Grades: No.1 | No.2
Sizes: Boilers | Small | Medium | Jumbo | Colossal
Packs: 2# | 1.36kg/3# | 2.72kg/5# | 10# | 25# | 40# | 50#
Store: Refrigerated | Optimum Temperature +1C/33F
Onions Overview: Page 131

Remarks: Easy to handle. White onions break down quickly, store in the cooler to help avoid this. Shrink can be substantial compared to the red and yellow varieties. Sales do not warrant retailing pre-packaged bags.

Displaying: Dummy displays for easy culling and restocking. Heaping displays is not recommended. Displaying red, white and yellow onions together and cross-selling will increase sales. There will be times when the tips look dried out and brown; it may be necessary to cut the tips with a pair of scissors to maintain steady sales. Time consuming, only do this if you have extra time available. Cull distressed product, bag up and discount.

Receiving: An entire shipment of white onions can breakdown overnight, once quality problems become apparent. Product should arrive dry, if the bags or boxes are wet...smell for a strong onion aroma (a sign of decay). Inspect stems for wetness, mold and press firmly at the base. White onions should be hard. Wet stems and black discoloration are signs of bad quality and should be rejected. Mold around the roots may also be evident. Reject moldy or sprouting onions and shipments in general with an accumulation of more than 10% defects.

Onions Yellow

Grades: No.1 | No.2
Sizes: Boilers | Small | Medium | Jumbo | Colossal
Packs: 2# | 1.36kg/3# | 2.72kg/5# | 10# | 25# | 40# | 50#
Store: Refrigerated | Optimum Temperature +1C/33F
Onions Overview: Page 131

Remarks: Normal yellow varieties are easy to handle. "Sweets" require extra attention because shrink can be substantial. Bagged onions are a critical part of sales, however listing bagged "sweets" is usually a very bad choice (onions rot in the bags, attract fruit flies and slow overall onion sales).

Displaying: Dummy displays for easy culling and restocking. Onions can be heaped with little impact. Displaying red, white and yellow onions together and cross-selling will increase sales. There will be times when the tips look dried out and brown; it may be necessary to cut the tips with a pair of scissors to maintain steady sales. Time consuming, only do this if you have extra time available. Cull distressed product, bag up and discount.

Receiving: Product should arrive dry, if the bags or boxes are wet...smell for a strong onion aroma (a sign of decay). Store Sweet onions in the cooler. Press your thumb against the surface, onions should feel very firm. Soft onions are old or may have been chilled. Inspect for mold (especially at the stem and root) and sprouting. Reject moldy or sprouting onions and shipments in general with an accumulation of more than 10% defects.

Ornamental Gourds / Corn

Grades: No U.S. or International
Gourds: Sold by Count & Weight | 18# Standard
Corn: Mini 12/3's | Large 12's Standard
Store: Unrefrigerated | Room Temperature

Gourds: Unwaxed gourds break down quickly, while waxed or shellacked product holds up indefinitely. Usually, there is no price difference (some growers wax, while others do not). Gourds can be heaped without impact and should be mixed with mini pumpkins, indian corn and strawberry popcorn for eye appeal and to maximize sales.

- Gourds – pound
- Mini pumpkins - pound or each
- Indian corn – each
- Strawberry popcorn – bunch (3's).

Indian corn and Strawberry popcorn kernels will fall off if handled roughly (the corn husks too). Hand place on gourd and mini pumpkin displays, keep inventory tight.

Receiving: Product does not sell after Thanksgiving, keep inventory light and manageable. Reduce and get rid of any remaining inventory the day before Thanksgiving. Easy enough to receive…reject gourds with decay spots, shrivelled stems or if they feel hollow. Corn with moldy leaves, missing kernels or husks will not sell either.

Parsnips

Grades: No.1 | No.2
Sizes: Medium | Jumbo
Bags: 1# | 2# | 1.36kg/3# | 2.72kg/5# | 10# | 20# | 25# | 50#
Store: Refrigerated | Optimum Temperature +1C/33F

Remarks: Easy to handle. Parsnips are usually harvested after the first Hard frost, making them sweeter and the veins softer. There are significant quality differences between No.1 and No.2 grades. No.2 grade can be tough, over-mature, oversized, have split stalks or fat tops with skinny bottoms (bottoms too skinny to be peeled). I recommend listing No.1 grade only. During Thanksgiving week, parsnip sales can increase +500%.

Displaying: Parsnips dry out quickly and should be displayed on a wet counter. Bulk parsnips should be trimmed, displays kept small and rotated regularly. Do not over-trim tops, you may need to re-trim them again later on. Turn off sprayers if you are retailing cello bags. Sales are limited, quantity pricing does not significantly increase tonnage.

Receiving: Weigh bulk bags. Inspect for split tips, mold and green shoots sprouting around the stem (all signs of age). During winter months a small percentage of defects is to be expected. Parsnips should be bright, clean and feel heavy. Cut open and check cores for black discoloration. Bunched parsnips should have green leaves, smell fresh and be medium to large size. Reject shipments in general with an accumulation of more than 10% defects.

Peas Green/Snow & Snap

Grades: Fancy | No.1
Cartons: 4.54kg/10# | 9kg/20# | 11.36kg/25#
Bags: 200g | 8oz | 1# | 2# | 1.36kg/3# | 2.72kg/5#
Store: Refrigerated | Optimum Temperature +1C/33F

Green Peas (aka Sweet or English): Peas are available seasonally and have a limited shelf-life. 2-3 days after harvest, peas will begin to taste old and stale. Sooner if the product was not cooled properly after being picked. Taste is everything. Dummy displays and rotate regularly.

Receiving: Always check the weight and remove the plastic pallet wrap to prevent sweating. Inspect peas for hail damage, wrinkling, mold and decay. Pea pods should be full and look attractive. Insert your hand into the box, if the peas feel warm to hot...the product was not cooled sufficiently after harvest and will breakdown within hours (so will boxes of wet peas). Sampling is the best test; ensure they taste sweet and fresh.

Snow/Snap Peas: Display on cold or wet counter (turn off sprayers). Packaged peas are best because they have an incredibly long shelf life. Mostly trouble free if good on arrival. Rotate regularly as you refill displays.

Receiving: Open packages, inspect for wrinkling, brown decay spots and mold. Pea tips should be light-green not turning brown. Cello packages should be clean and free of condensation. Reject shipments in general with an accumulation of more than 10% defects.

Peppers Overview

There are countless varieties of peppers available; we will discuss the most popular varieties and colors. Easy to handle, the biggest problem Produce Clerks face is receiving poor quality. Recognizing defects will help you understand that the blame quite often…is solely on the grower's inability to deliver you a good product.

Peppers should be harvested hard and crisp like apples. Greenhouse products tend to meet this criteria, however there are wide-ranging differences when we look at field grown peppers. Supermarkets buying strictly on price are usually purchasing second-rate quality (whether they realize or not). In this case, quality standards are usually poor for two good reasons… producers are not going to take extra care packing peppers at bottom prices… or they are just bad growers. The best growers like to develop their labels (e.g. Dole, Master's Touch, Sun World, etc.) and generally good labels cost a bit more.

<u>Colored Peppers</u>

Many supermarkets carry greenhouse grown bell peppers because generally they are better quality. Growers have higher grading standards and questionable peppers are culled and sold as no.2 grade. Bell pepper varieties have thicker walls which translates into a much longer shelf-life compared to most field grown varieties.

During summer months however, it is a good idea to list field grown too. At this time of year many European shoppers purchase large volumes for grilling, canning and pickling. Regular customers turn to local Farmer's Markets when their supermarkets do not offer a choice. Field peppers can cost substantially less (up to +100%) than greenhouse products. It is important to remain competitive during the "Locally Grown" season and shoppers love it when supermarkets support local growers. Include a realistic case price on your signage.

Popular Caselot Varieties

- Red Peppers (sweet)
- Green Peppers (sweet)
- Red Sheppard Peppers (sweet)
- Red Pimento Peppers (sweet)
- Yellow Hungarian Peppers (sweet)
- Rings of Fire Chili Peppers (hot)
- Cayenne Chili Peppers (hot)

Other Caselot Varieties

- Yellow Apple Peppers (hot)
- Yellow Dove Peppers (sweet)
- Red Crimson Peppers (hot)
- Red Cherry Peppers (hot)
- Red Goat Horn Peppers (hot)
- Red Super Sheppard Peppers (sweet)
- Purple Peppers (sweet)
- Orange Pimento Peppers (sweet)

Green Peppers

Green peppers are commonly received with soft defects. Purchasers without retail experience may not realize how much product is being culled and thrown out when peppers are bought solely on price (even No.1 grade). Having them visit the store occasionally will change that. Cull percentages can be substantial. Stick with good labels.

Hot Peppers

Jalapeno are usually the only mover in the Produce section. Most supermarkets may not even offer any other variety besides Jalapeno. The Poblano, Serrano, Scotch Bonnet, Habanero and Anaheim varieties are also popular. This category generally loses money and culling can be excessive, but hot peppers are becoming more popular.

Having a small specialty pepper section is a good idea. Putting up a copy of the "Scoleville Hot Pepper Scale" will increase sales, reduce culls and have interested shoppers buying and trying new varieties. Remember to wear gloves when handling hot peppers, do not rub your eyes and wash your hands before taking a washroom break.

If you are a typical gung-ho Produce Clerk and into sampling hot peppers, milk eases the pain.

Peppers Green

Grades: Fancy | No.1 | No.2 (Choice or Choppers)
Sizes: Small | Medium | Large | X-Large | Jumbo
Cartons: 11.36-12.73kg/25-28# Standard
Bags: 4ct | 2# | 1.36kg/3# **Bins:** 182kg/400# | 364kg/800#
Store: Refrigerated | Optimum Temperature +1C/33F
Peppers Overview: Page 140

Remarks: Easy to handle. No.1 grade peppers should be carried to keep culls and shrink in check. Large sell best.

Displaying: Peppers will roll onto the floor, crack and split open if stacked too high. Widen displays instead during peak times. Dummying table displays will reduce culls. Rotate regularly. Retailing green and colored varieties together will increase sales. Peppers are often waxed, displaying under hot light fixtures can make them feel greasy... slowing sales. Cull soft, wrinkled, waxy and cracked peppers. Bag up (mix colors) and sell at a discount. Throw out decayed peppers.

Receiving: Boxes that have an overpowering pepper aroma usually have quality problems (check boxes for wet bottoms). Weigh boxes. Open and inspect for mold, bruises, cracks, pock-marks and deformities. Peppers should feel hard, clean, smooth-skinned and the stems green not black (sometimes there is slime and wetness around the base of the stem). No.1 grade should be uniform in shape not deformed. Product that feels greasy will not sell well. Reject shipments in general with an accumulation of more than 10% defects.

Peppers Colored

Grades: Fancy|No.1|No.2 (Choice or Choppers)
Sizes: Small|Medium|Large|X-Large|Jumbo
Cartons: 5kg/11#|6.82kg/15#|11.36-12.73kg/25-28#
Bags: 3ct|4ct|2#|1.36kg/3#
Store: Refrigerated|Optimum Temperature +1C/33F
Peppers Overview: Page 140

Remarks: Easy to handle. No.1 grade peppers should be carried to keep culls and shrink in check. Large sell best.

Displaying: Peppers will roll onto the floor, crack and split open if stacked too high. Widen displays instead during peak times. Dummying table displays will reduce culls. Rotate regularly. Retailing colored and green varieties together will increase sales. Peppers are often waxed, displaying under hot light fixtures can make them feel greasy... slowing sales. Cull soft, wrinkled, waxy and cracked peppers. Bag up (mix colors) and sell at a discount. Throw out decayed peppers.

Receiving: Boxes that have an overpowering pepper aroma usually have quality problems (check boxes for wet bottoms). Weigh boxes. Open and inspect for mold, bruises, cracks, pock-marks and deformities. Peppers should feel hard, clean, smooth-skinned and the stems green not black (sometimes there is slime and wetness around the base of the stem). No.1 grade should be uniform in shape not deformed. Product that feels greasy will not sell well. Reject shipments in general with an accumulation of more than 10% defects.

Potatoes Overview

The potato category is relative easy to handle, unless product is received with pre-existing quality problems. It is actually surprising how common poor quality is shipped and received. Receivers usually give potatoes the obligatory cursory glance and move on. Unscrupulous packers count on this.

Green Potatoes

More prevalent to yellow and white skinned varieties, dummying displays and proper rotation will help reduce shrink. Do not display under bright halogen track lighting and completely cover potato displays with dark tarps (to keep light out) at close.

Black Flesh

More a problem associated with winter storage potatoes than new crop (russet potatoes especially). Although both new and old crop can be affected. Black skin discoloration can be an indicator the problem is more serious. Cut open and inspect flesh.

Silver Scurf

Silver scabbing on the skin of the potato does not affect the flesh, but is ugly enough to deter sales.

Creamer Potatoes

Baby potatoes, also referred to as "creamers" are an important part of potato sales. Bulk (loose) sales are usually limited and the potatoes dry out quickly. New-dug varieties with thin skins will also turn green within hours on display. It is a better idea to offer pre-bagged packages (1lb, 2lb, 3lb or 5lb bags) and quantity pricing will increase sales significantly.

Creamers suffer from the same quality defects as regular sized potatoes, but are more noticeable. Yellow-fleshed and white skinned varieties have thinner skins which make them better eating.

Receiving

Unscrupulous packers will mix No.2 grade or "B" sized potatoes into No.1 grade "A" sized potato bags. Deformed, pock-marked and spotted potatoes are also common defects you may find upon closer inspection.

Supporting local producers is important and at certain times of year…quality can be mixed. As a general rule, the shipments are acceptable if your customers continue to purchase the product without complaint; and you are not throwing out excessive amounts of potatoes.

Otherwise, the Packer should be advised to improve their packing standards or face possible de-listing. If you are buying strictly on price, quality problems will persist.

Potatoes Red

Grades: No.1 | No.2
Sizes: A (Large) | B (Medium) | C (Creamers)
Cartons: 22.73kg/50# Standard
Bags: 2# | 1.36kg/3# | 2.27kg/5# | 4.54kg/10# | 9kg/20#
Store: Refrigerated | Optimum Temperature +1C/33F
Potatoes Overview: Page 145

Remarks: Easy to handle. Red potatoes are recommended for potato salads because of their firmer flesh. Their thick skins also give them an excellent shelf-life on displays.

Displaying: Reds potatoes can be stacked several layers high without impact. The majority of sales are 10lb bags and should be allocated table space accordingly. Quantity pricing increases sales. Light does turn potatoes green (inedible), try not to display in bright areas of the produce department. Cover displays with dark tarps at close to reduce "greening" and extend their shelf-life. Cull soft, dried, wrinkled, cracked and green potatoes and sell cheap.

Receiving: Rotting potatoes have a terrible odor that can often be noticed throughout the entire store.
Always smell bags and boxes. Inspect for green color, black discoloration, silver scurf, cracks and spotting. Wrinkling can be a sign of age or chilling injury. Potatoes should be hard. Store covered to prevent greening. Winter storage and baby potatoes hold up better in the cooler. Reject shipments in general with an accumulation of more than 10% defects.

Potatoes Russet/White

Grades: No.1 | No.2
Sizes: A (Large) | B (Medium) | C (Creamers)
Cartons: 22.73kg/50# Standard
Bags: 2# | 1.36kg/3# | 2.27kg/5# | 4.54kg/10# | 9kg/20#
Store: Refrigerated | Optimum Temperature +1C/33F
Potatoes Overview: Page 145

Remarks: Easy to handle. Russets are recommended for french fries, baked and mashed potatoes because of their fluffiness. Whites have thinner skins and are good eating with their skins on; and boiled or mashed too.

Displaying: Russets can be heaped, while Whites turn green easily. The majority of sales are 10lb bags and table space should be allocated accordingly. Quantity pricing increases sales. Light does turn potatoes green (inedible), try not to display in bright areas of the produce department. Cover displays with dark tarps at close to reduce "greening" and extend their shelf-life. Cull soft, dried, wrinkled, cracked and green potatoes and sell cheap.

Receiving: Rotting potatoes, have a terrible odor that can often be noticed throughout the entire store.
Always smell bags and boxes. Inspect for green color, black discoloration, silver scurf, cracks and spotting. Wrinkling can be a sign of age or chilling injury. Potatoes should be hard. Store covered to prevent greening. White varieties (including baby) should always be stored refrigerated. Reject shipments in general with an accumulation of more than 10% defects.

Potatoes Yellow

Grades: No.1 | No.2
Sizes: A (Large) | B (Medium) | C (Creamers)
Cartons: 22.73kg/50# Standard
Bags: 2# | 1.36kg/3# | 2.27kg/5# | 4.54kg/10# | 9kg/20#
Store: Refrigerated | Optimum Temperature +1C/33F
Potatoes Overview: Page 145

Remarks: Sometimes difficult to handle (prone to greening). Yellow-fleshed Yukon Gold and Bintje are favorite varieties. Recommended for stuffings and mashed potatoes because of their buttery flavor and fluffiness.

Displaying: Keep displays dummied. Usually priced higher than red, russet and white; 5lb bags may outsell other pack sizes. Quantity pricing increases sales. Light does turn potatoes green (inedible), try not to display in bright areas of the produce department. Cover displays with dark tarps at close to reduce "greening" and extend their shelf-life. Cull soft, dried, wrinkled, cracked and green potatoes and sell cheap.

Receiving: Rotting potatoes, have a terrible odor that can often be noticed throughout the entire store.
Always smell bags and boxes. Inspect for green color, black discoloration, silver scurf, cracks and spotting. Wrinkling can be a sign of age or chilling injury. Potatoes should be hard. Keep refrigerated and store covered to prevent greening. Reject shipments in general with an accumulation of more than 10% defects.

Pumpkins

Grades: No.1 | No.2
Bags: 11.36kg/25# | 18kg/40# | 22.73kg/50#
Bins: 364kg/800# | 454kg/1000#
Store: Refrigerated | Optimum Temperature +1C/33F

Remarks: There are eating pumpkins and decorative pumpkins. Most supermarkets offer Pie pumpkins at Thanksgiving but otherwise do not list eating varieties. Decorative varieties are only offered for Halloween.

Decorative Pumpkins: Decorative varieties are critical to supermarkets during Halloween month. Large family-sized and kid-sized need to be kept in stock. Big displays are encouraged as long as they are manageable. Damaged pumpkins can be reduced and marketed for quick sale as "Ugly Pumpkins". Mold is common and spreads quickly, throw out decaying pumpkins.

Eating Pumpkins: Eating varieties are sweet and taste similar to squash. Pumpkins have a strong shelf-life. It is normal to receive these varieties greenish-orange and they can be eaten straight away. Product will wrinkle, loss mass and turn completely orange as it ages. Eaten widely by Caribbean and African peoples.

Receiving: Inspect around stem base and butt for decay, mold and mushy flesh. Pumpkins should feel firm and heavy. Stems extend shelf-life and should be firmly attached (shoppers will not purchase decorative pumpkins unless their stem is attached). Store extra stock in cooler.

Radishes

Grades: No.1 | Commercial
Bunched: 24ct | 48ct
Cello Bags: 6oz | 1# | 11.36kg/25# Bulk
Store: Refrigerated | Optimum Temperature +1C/33F

Remarks: Unless there is a quality problem, Radish sales remain steady. Cello packages have a strong shelf-life, while bunched are a money losing write-off. Quantity pricing is ideal.

Bunched Radishes: Display on a wet counter for best results. Keep displays minimized. Rotate regularly or product will become drenched from sprayers. Bunches begin to stink as their leaves break down. Cull drenched, decaying and smelly bunches and throw out.

Cello Radishes: Easy to handle. Display on a wet counter (turn off sprayers). Cello radishes can be stacked several layers high with little impact. While restocking, you will have to occasionally shake bags to get rid of condensation. Cull packages with green shoots, black discoloration or cracked radishes and discount.

Receiving: Check "Best Before" date on cello packages. Product should be clean, bright and feel firm. Old radishes will often have green shoots or white cracks (frozen appearance) throughout their flesh. Bunched radishes will stink as they break down. Smell the boxes, yellow leaves or decay around the elastic bands/ties are signs of age. Reject stinky shipments and shipments in general with an accumulation of more than 10% defects.

Purple-Top Rutabagas/Turnips

Grades: No.1 | No.2 | Unclassified
Bags: 4.54kg/10# | 11.36kg/25# | 22.73kg/50#
Store: Refrigerated | Optimum Temperature +1C/33F

Rutabagas: Easy to handle, Rutabaga sales remain steady. These yellow-fleshed varieties are typically harvested after the first Hard frost (killing hard veins and making the flesh sweeter and tender). Rutabagas are a winter root crop that can be stored for extremely long periods near zero.

Turnips: White-fleshed summer varieties are sweeter and very popular among Middle-Eastern peoples. They do not hold up as well on display, rotate regularly to reduce culls.

Displaying: Rutabagas and turnips are secondary items that should be displayed on a wet counter. Keep displays small. Trim tops when stocking displays (bottoms too if required), over-trimming will slow sales. Medium sized sell better.

Receiving: Inspect for mold and scabbing on the surface. A small percentage of green shoots is okay, they can be trimmed. Flesh should be clean, black discoloration of the ring is a sign of age and should be rejected. White-fleshed turnips with black discoloration on their skin will not sell. Reject shipments in general with an accumulation of more than 10% defects.

Spinach

Grades: Extra No.1 | No.1 | Commercial
Bunched: 24ct Standard
Bags: 10oz | 1# | 2# | 1.14kg/2.5# | 1.36kg/3#
Store: Refrigerated | Optimum Temperature +1C/33F

Remarks: Shoppers are very picky when it comes to spinach, sales can be erratic.

Bunched Spinach: Display on a wet counter. Trimmed bunches (rootless) are cleaner and easier to work with; but their shelf-life is shorter when their roots are removed. Regular bunches are often full of soil and messy to handle; but the longer shelf-life may make it worthwhile. Pre-soak bunches in a sink of cold water to remove excess soil and crisp up the leaves. Rotate regularly to avoid sprayers drenching bunches. Quantity pricing improves sales.

Cello Spinach: Easy to handle, display on a cold counter. Bags have an excellent shelf-life, while restocking you may have to occasionally shake bags to get rid of condensation. Rotate regularly. Cull packages with yellow or decayed leaves, discount and sell cheap.

Receiving: Inspect for clods of soil, yellowing and decayed leaves. Bunches should be clean and look full, with crisp leaves (not wilted). Check "Best Before" date on cello packages. Condensation is a sign the product has been sitting out too long or the truck driver turned off the reefer. Inspect closely. Reject shipments in general with an accumulation of more than 10% defects.

Squash Hard-shell

Grades: No.1 | No.2
Cartons: 11.36kg/25# | 18kg/40#
Bins: 364kg/800# | 454kg/1000#
Popular: Butternut | Spaghetti | Buttercup | Kabocha
Store: Refrigerated | Optimum Temperature +1C/33F

Remarks: Easy to handle. Acorn, Hubbard and Turban varieties are very slow sellers. Butternut is most popular, followed by Kabocha (Japanese), Buttercup and Spaghetti. More popular during winter months, hard-shell squash can be stored for extremely long periods near zero.

Displaying: Having a "mix n' match" table display works best. Squash can be heaped with little impact. Rotate at least once daily. Ensuring you have Butternut is key to a successful "mix n' match" display. Displaying squash under hot light fixtures will turn them waxy and sales will drop off. Cull soft, waxy and wrinkled squash. Bag up and sell cheap. Decayed squash should be thrown out.

Receiving: Squash breakdown faster if their stems are missing. Weigh boxes. Spaghetti squash are regularly shipped moldy and decayed, open boxes and check bottom layers closely. The biggest problem with Butternut is missing stems, while Kabocha and Buttercup are usually fine. Check for excessive scabbing, mold, decay and wrinkling. Reject shipments missing their stems and shipments in general with an accumulation of more than 10% defects.

Squash Zucchini

Grades: No.1 | No.2
Sizes: Extra Fancy | Fancy | Medium
Cartons: 10kg/22# | 18kg/40#
Store: Refrigerated | Optimum Temperature +5-10C/41-50F

Remarks: Many types fall under the "summer squash" category, Zucchini being the most popular. Patty Pan, Yellow Crookneck and Cousa are also popular varieties. Susceptible to chilling, do not store summer squash in front of cooler fans. You may want to keep covered or wrapped in plastic pallet wrap to avoid chilling injury.

Displaying: Product should be displayed on a wet counter. Large table displays are feasible if the product is regularly sprayed down (keep a water spray bottle close by). Stems should be lightly trimmed, do not over-trim (you may have to trim again later on). Carrying Medium size usually translates into less culling. Zucchini will get soft, pitted and their skin will start to decay if product is not rotated regularly. Dummy table displays during slow times or move to the wet counter.

Receiving: Open boxes and inspect stems for mold, wetness and decay. Run your fingers firmly along the surface to ensure skin is not loose or slimy. Check butt ends for decay spots, sticky puss and brown discoloration. Dried-out flower blooms attached to the butts is okay, but ensure they are removed when putting up stock. Reject soft squash and shipments in general with an accumulation of more than 10% defects.

Suey Choy/Napa Cabbage

Grades: No U.S. or International
Cartons: 4.54kg/10# | 9kg/20# | 25# | 30# | 40# | 50# | 70#
Store: Refrigerated | Optimum Temperature +1C/33F

Remarks: Easy to handle and more popular than Bok Choy. "Suey Choy" aka "Napa Cabbage" should be harvested light-green. Dark-green leaves are a sign of immaturity and will slow sales. All Asian peoples eat suey choy, but perhaps Koreans consume the largest quantities. Suey choy is the main ingredient of the Korean staple, spicy, pickled Kimchee.

Displaying: Price sensitive, overcharging will stifle sales. Display on a wet counter. Lightly trim butts and remove any damaged leaves while stocking display. Product should be sold banded, taped or over-wrapped. Suey choy has an excellent shelf-life. Cull dark-green, wilted or spotted product. Bag up and sell cheap.

Receiving: Open boxes and inspect for tip burn, color, black spots along the stalks, and insect damage. Black spotting (old age) and insect damage are common defects. Suey choy heads should be clean with tight, compact leaves. Peel back outer leaves and inspect closely for insect infestation. Reject shipments with dark-green leaves and shipments in general with an accumulation of more than 10% defects.

Tomato Overview

Tomatoes are huge part of the Produce Department. Culling and shrink can be significant. Following a few simple procedures will reduce the time spent managing displays and losses.

<u>Receiving & Storage</u>

Press your thumb gently against the flesh… tomatoes should be received firm (slightly soft is okay). Soft tomatoes and fruit showing signs of wrinkling or flat shoulders are indicators of overripe stock. Dried green stems is a sign of old age.

Once product starts to breakdown in the box, the acid in tomatoes will rapidly affect and break down the rest of the box. Inspect around the stem bowl closely…this is where the onset of decay usually begins.

Blight can be a serious problem too (green and yellow splotches on the skin). Tomatoes with "Blight" look ugly, will not ripen and should be rejected.

Fruit that looks good but feels overly soft could be a sign of chilling by the truck reefer. If the delivery vehicle does not have a warm compartment to hold tomatoes in-transit…the product should be wrapped in plastic pallet wrap and covered to prevent chilling.

Field tomatoes produce an excessive amount of ethylene gas (page 27, diagram 6B). Ethylene is a naturally occurring gas that induces ripening. To slow down the ripening process remove tomato box lids and plastic pallet wrap. This will extend tomato shelf-life.

The opposite method should be applied if the tomatoes are greenish or pink. Keep lids closed and ensure the pallet is wrapped with plastic pallet wrap. This method causes the fruit to sweat and traps the ethylene gas, speeding up the ripening process.

Tomatoes should never be refrigerated. Ripe tomatoes will especially become chilled and damaged by the cold temperatures. If you become backed up with ripe fruit, bagging or basketing (4-6ct), or offering by the Caselot for "canning" is always a viable option. Shoppers are always looking for ripe tomatoes. Usually you can still sell the product at a profit (0-100%).

Displaying

Tomatoes are fragile and should be handled gently. Dumping tomatoes onto displays will cause significant damage and usually means more culling later on. Sometimes the damage is not apparent until after the customer has gotten the product home. Dummying displays makes rotation much easier and efficient. Use apple pads or similar pads to cushion the bottom layer of tomatoes and reduce losses (page 14, diagram 3C). Ripe fruit should be displayed on top and green product kept in the back-room to ripen further. During peak times, displays can be widened out instead of being heaped (reducing culls and shrink further). Display beside cucumbers and peppers to increase sales or move excess inventory.

When tomatoes are pink, advise shoppers they can speed up the ripening process by storing tomatoes on the kitchen counter in a tied plastic bag (two is better). The bag traps the ethylene gas.

Grape & Cherry Tomatoes

Usually marketed in one pint clamshells. Grape tomatoes outsell Cherry tomatoes at least 2-to-1. Ripe red tomatoes should be displayed on top layers and moved quickly. You may need to remove the occasional wrinkled tomato from a clamshell to ensure steady sales.

Grape and Cherry tomatoes sell significantly better when quantity priced. Mix-n-match is a good idea.

These varieties are normally pre-ripened and over ordering can cause problems. Having a maximum 2-3 day supply should suffice. Product harvested with their green stems attached have a better shelf-life. Ensure the stems are not dried out or moldy when they are received.

Tomatoes Field

Grades: No.1 | No.2 | Canning
Sizes: 4x4 | 4x5 | 5x5 | 5x6 | 6x6 | 6x7 | 7x7
Sizes: Small | Medium | Large | Extra Large
Cartons: 10kg/22# 2-3 Layer | 11.36kg/25# Volume Fill
Store: Unrefrigerated | Optimum Temperature +10C/50F
Tomato Overview: Page 157

Remarks: Field-grown tomatoes are the most popular and "Beefsteak" varieties sell best. Adding the blurb "BEEFSTEAK" to your signage will increase sales. Shoppers are typically picky when it comes to tomatoes.

Displaying: Dummy displays to reduce culling and keep displays fresh (page 14, diagram 3C). Do not dump. Tomatoes with green stems will cause stem punctures. Field varieties are normally coated with a wax or vegetable oil to extend their longevity; displaying under hot light fixtures can make them feel greasy and sales will slow. Sampling tasty beefsteak varieties will also increase sales. Cull soft, waxy or wrinkled fruit, bag up and sell at a discount. Overripe product can be sold in large bags or cases as "Canning Tomatoes".

Receiving: Review "Receiving" on page 157. Inspect around the stem bowl…if there are signs of mold, decay and wetness in the box, rapid breakdown of the remaining fruit is usually imminent. Press your thumb gently against the shoulder skin to ensure it does not peel away. Check for softness, chilling and blight. Reject waxy or greasy tomato shipments and shipments in general with an accumulation of more than 10% defects.

Tomatoes Greenhouse

Grades: No.1 | No.2 | Canning
Sizes: Small | Medium | Large | Extra Large
Cartons: 4.54kg/10# | 5kg/11# | 6.82kg/15# | 9kg/20#
Store: Unrefrigerated | Optimum Temperature +10C/50F
Tomato Overview: Page 157

Remarks: "Greenhouse" aka "Hot House" tomatoes are more expensive and better quality. Most growers have switched to more flavorful varieties, which has improved sales. Adding the blurb "Beefsteak" or "Heirloom" variety to your signage will increase sales. Shoppers are typically picky when it comes to tomatoes. Rotate regularly. Bag up culls and discount or as cases of canning tomatoes.

Displaying: Greenhouse tomatoes have fragile shoulders, dummy displays (page 14, diagram 3C). Single-layer trays are best. Stacking more than 2-3 layers high can cause significant stem puncture damage. "Tomatoes on the vine" aka "Tov's" should be stacked no more than 2 layers high. Fruit falling off the vines is a good indicator the tomatoes need to be moved quickly.

Receiving: Review "Receiving" on page 157. Inspect around the stem bowl...if there are signs of mold, decay and wetness in the box, rapid breakdown of the remaining fruit is usually imminent. Press your thumb gently against the shoulder skin to ensure it does not peel away. Dried stems and vines mean the fruit is old. Check for softness and chilling. Reject shipments in general with an accumulation of more than 10% defects.

Yams/Sweet Potatoes

Grades: Extra No.1 | No.1 | No.1 Petite | Commercial | No.2
Sizes: Small | Medium | Large | Jumbo | Mixed
Cartons: 4.54kg/10# | 9kg/20# | 18kg/40# Standard
Bins: 454kg/1000# | 545kg/1200#
Store: Unrefrigerated | Optimum Temperature +10C/50F

Remarks: Most varieties of Yams grown in the U.S. are actually Sweet Potatoes. We distinguish the two major commercially grown types by labelling "orange-fleshed" as Yams and "white-fleshed" as Sweet Potatoes.

Displaying: Easy to handle. Trimming the tips causes the product to mold and breakdown. Yams can be heaped with little impact, however is not warranted except during the Thanksgiving and Christmas seasons. Cull broken and black discolored pieces and sell cheap.

Receiving: Sweet Potatoes and Yams are very dense, dropping boxes on the floor will cause them to break. It is common to receive decayed product but sometimes hard to notice unless you look very closely (quite often the color remains the same). Inspect for chilling injury, especially "orange-fleshed" (black discoloration). "White-fleshed" may look particularly ugly with lots of black markings. Reject shipments in general with an accumulation of more than 10% defects.

Afterword

This guide needs to be used with a little bit of common sense and ask your supervisor for clarification when necessary. Contact me or post a question or comment on my website if you cannot get a clear answer. I am often travelling on business somewhere in the world and internet and phone service is not always readily available. Be patient and I will get back to you.

Rejecting shipments of produce is not always an option and weather related issues are often uncontrollable. Sometimes it's enough to make a notation on the Bill of Lading for future reference or contacting the warehouse, grower or shipper and asking for credit. In the long run… working together is in everyone's best interest.

Produce Buyers and Management without RETAIL experience cannot always understand your problems. They may wave them off casually without any regard to your abilities or feelings. Sometimes you need to speak up, but remember…try to play nice!

The produce business is one of camaraderie, it crosses borders and has a global reach. Handling and Retailing produce is a skill that is always in demand.

PRODUCE CLERKS ARE IN DEMAND!

ABOUT THE AUTHOR

Rick Chong started in the produce business in May, 1984. He has worked all facets of the Produce Industry. Winning several awards for retail excellence.

- Picker
- Receiver
- Trucker
- Off-Shore Buyer
- Field Inspector
- Warehouse Manager
- Retailer
- National Foodservice Produce Manager
- National Retail Produce Manager
- Importer
- Exporter
- Grower
- Packer
- Sales Manager

Currently Sales Manager & Partner in Sutherland S.A. Produce headquartered in British Columbia, Canada. Specializing in the growing, packing and exporting of fresh cherries world-wide.

Made in the USA
Las Vegas, NV
15 January 2023

65656085R00104